Visions from
San Francisco Bay

Czeslaw Milosz
Visions from San Francisco Bay

Translated by Richard Lourie

Farrar Straus Giroux

New York

Translation copyright © 1975, 1982
by Farrar, Straus and Giroux, Inc.
Originally published by Institut Littéraire in
Polish as *Widzenia nad Zatoka San Francisco*, 1969
All rights reserved
Published simultaneously in Canada by
McGraw-Hill Ryerson Ltd., Toronto
Printed in the United States of America
Designed by Laurel Wagner
First printing, 1982

Library of Congress Cataloging in Publication Data
Milosz, Czeslaw.
Visions from San Francisco Bay.
Translation of: Widzenia nad Zatoka San Francisco.
E169.12.M5513   1982   973.9   82–9215
                                     AACR2

Portions of this translation appeared, in slightly
different form, in *Dissent*, *The New Republic*,
Grand Street, and *The Ark 14 . . . For Rexroth*.
"To Robinson Jeffers" is from *Selected Poems* by
Czeslaw Milosz, copyright © 1973 by Czeslaw Milosz;
reprinted by permission of The Continuum Publishing
Corporation. Lines from "Howl" by Allen Ginsberg,
copyright © 1956, 1959 by Allen Ginsberg;
reprinted by permission of City Lights Books.
"Continent's End" by Robinson Jeffers, copyright 1924
and renewed 1952 by Robinson Jeffers; reprinted
from *The Selected Poetry of Robinson Jeffers*,
by permission of Random House, Inc. Translation of
"Emigration to America," first published in
different form, as "Biblical Heirs and Modern Evils"
(*The Immigrant Experience*; Thomas Wheeler, ed.,
Dial Press) © 1971 by Czeslaw Milosz; originally
published in Polish in *Kultura*, Paris, France, 1969

Contents

My Intention   3

Where I Am   6

Facing Too Large an Expanse   9

Symbolic Mountains and Forests   12

Remembrance of a Certain Love   17

On the Effects of the Natural Sciences   21

*A Short Digression on Woman as a Representative
    of Nature*   26

Religion and Space   30

A Certain Illness Difficult to Name   36

Migrations   41

The Events in California   45

On That Century   52

On the Western   57

I and They   62

The Image of the Beast   66

What Is Mine? 70

On the Turmoil of Many Religions 74

On Catholicism 81

Carmel 87

To Robinson Jeffers 95

Sex Provided 97

On Censorship 103

The Agony of the West 114

The Formless and the New 122

The Evangelical Emissary 132

Henry Miller 136

I, Motor, Earth 141

On Virtue 149

The Dance of Death and Human Inequality 160

*Essay in Which the Author Confesses That He Is on
        the Side of Man, for Lack of Anything Better* 172

The Rebirth of Utopia: Herbert Marcuse 184

Emigration to America: A Summing Up 198

Visions from
San Francisco Bay

My Intention

I am here. Those three words contain all that can be said—
you begin with those words and you return to them. Here
means on this earth, on this continent and no other, in this
city and no other, and in this epoch I call mine, this century, this year. I was given no other place, no other time,
and I touch my desk to defend myself against the feeling
that my own body is transient. This is all very fundamental,
but, after all, the science of life depends on the gradual
discovery of fundamental truths.

I have written on various subjects, and not, for the most
part, as I would have wished. Nor will I realize my long-
standing intention this time. But I am always aware that
what I want is impossible to achieve. I would need the
ability to communicate my full amazement at "being here"
in one unattainable sentence which would simultaneously
transmit the smell and texture of my skin, everything stored
in my memory, and all I now assent to, dissent from. However, in pursuing the impossible, I did learn something.
Each of us is so ashamed of his own helplessness and ignorance that he considers it appropriate to communicate
only what he thinks others will understand. There are,
however, times when somehow we slowly divest ourselves

of that shame and begin to speak openly about all the things we do not understand. If I am not wise, then why must I pretend to be? If I am lost, why must I pretend to have ready counsel for my contemporaries? But perhaps the value of communication depends on the acknowledgment of one's own limits, which, mysteriously, are also limits common to many others; and aren't these the same limits of a hundred or a thousand years ago? And when the air is filled with the clamor of analysis and conclusion, would it be entirely useless to admit you do not understand?

I have read many books, but to place all those volumes on top of one another and stand on them would not add a cubit to my stature. Their learned terms are of little use when I attempt to seize naked experience, which eludes all accepted ideas. To borrow their language can be helpful in many ways, but it also leads imperceptibly into a self-contained labyrinth, leaving us in alien corridors which allow no exit. And so I must offer resistance, check every moment to be sure I am not departing from what I have actually experienced on my own, what I myself have touched. I cannot invent a new language and I use the one I was first taught, but I can distinguish, I hope, between what is mine and what is merely fashionable. I cannot expel from memory the books I have read, their contending theories and philosophies, but I am free to be suspicious and to ask naïve questions instead of joining the chorus which affirms and denies.

Intimidation. I am brave and undaunted in the certainty of having something important to say to the world, something no one else will be called to say. Then the feeling of individuality and a unique role begins to weaken and the thought of all the people who ever were, are, and ever will be—aspiring, doubting, believing—people superior to me in strength of feeling and depth of mind, robs me of confidence in what I call my "I." The words of a prayer two millennia old, the celestial music created by a composer in a wig and jabot make me ask why I, too, am here, why me? Shouldn't one evaluate his chances beforehand—either equal the best or say nothing. Right at this moment, as I put these marks to paper, countless others are doing the same, and our books in their brightly colored jackets will be added to that mass of things in which names and titles sink and vanish. No doubt, also at this very moment, someone is standing in a bookstore and, faced with the sight of those splendid and vain ambitions, is making his decision—silence is better. That single phrase which, were it truly weighed, would suffice as a life's work. However, here, now, I have the courage to speak, a sort of secondary courage, not blind. Perhaps it is my stubbornness in pursuit of that single sentence. Or perhaps it is my old fearlessness, temperament, fate, a search for a new dodge. In any case, my consolation lies not so much in the role I have been called on to play as in the great mosaic-like whole which is composed of the fragments of various people's efforts, whether successful or not. I am here—and everyone is in some "here"—and the only thing we can do is try to communicate with one another.

Where I Am

It has been said that the problems that face California today, America must meet tomorrow. The waves of the future break first on the rocky California coast, change comes most rapidly. There is truth in this. It misses the point a little, because no place is like any other place, and California is in many ways unique. Yet no one can afford to be unaware of the changes and difficulties that confront California. They are too likely to be the problems of all the civilized world.

Raymond F. Dasmann, *The Destruction of California*

Walking along the street, I raise my eyes and see the nuclear laboratories glowing among the eucalyptus trees in the folds of a hill. I turn, and there is San Francisco Bay, metallic and darkening now, taking only some of the sky's green, yellow, and carmine. Berkeley clings to hills which face west, toward the Pacific, and its best hours—afternoon, dusk, the famous sunsets, evening—are unspoiled by sea fog. There are many cities and countries in my mind, but they all stand in relation to the one which surrounds me every day. The human imagination is spatial and it is constantly constructing an architectonic whole from landscapes remembered or imagined; it progresses from what is closest to what is farther away, winding layers or strands around the single axis, which begins where the feet touch the ground. Many consequences flow from the spatial nature of the imagination, and I will return to them frequently. Now I will limit myself to saying that for me, awake or dreaming, the four corners of the world begin with the forms almost within reach of my hand. To the west, the islands and promontories of the bay, the bridges —two dinosaurs—San Francisco's clustered skyscrapers, the Golden Gate flaring and fading in the regular intervals of light on steel threads too fine to be seen, and, beyond the bridge, the open sea. To the east, roads that follow the cliffs, the eucalyptus trees on the slopes, scree the color of a rattlesnake, a tunnel, and empty hills banked up to the horizon—pale green hills tending to rose and violet for a few months a year, then flaxen under the brilliant blue sky, rarely reached by the fog from the sea. To the south, a flat sterile plane inhabited by a million people, the city of Oakland, and above it, the elliptical concrete bands which lead southward to San Jose and Los Angeles. The north, too, is marked by bands bearing three lanes of traffic toward the wine country around Napa and Santa Rosa, and then come the coniferous forests of northern California, where eagles circle above chasms of mist.

My imagination does not venture very far west, where there is nothing but thousands of miles of ocean forever the same; nor does it roam farther east than the Sacramento Valley and its pass in the Sierra Nevadas. Past the Sierra Nevadas it encounters a zero—the empty, wrinkled surface of the planet crossed by jets in a matter of hours. On the other hand, my imagination likes to play with images—it constantly shifts the great deserts of southern California and Arizona, rearranges the rocks (cathedrals? petrified, primeval lizards?) jutting out from the water by the wild Oregon coast, and toys with the orchards in Washington near the Mt. Rainier glacier.

No, picture postcards in prose are not my specialty. But still I find something oppressive in the virginity of this country, virgin in the sense that it seems to be waiting for its names. America was not slowly and gradually put into words over the centuries; and if somebody tried to render it in words, the changes were so great, twenty years much the equal of two hundred elsewhere, that the slate was always being wiped clean. Both here, on the West Coast, and everywhere in America, one is faced with something that is impossible to define by allusions to the "humanistically formed imagination"—something incomprehensible in regard both to the forms taken in by the eye and to the attempt to connect those forms to the lives of human beings. Our species is now on a mad adventure. We are flung into a world which appears to be a nothing, or, at best, a chaos of disjointed masses we must arrange in some order, in some relation to one another—this to the right of that, that to the left of this—using a map's abstract planes. The disturbing freedom of encountering a plateau, river canyon, or crater where nobody has been before or has at least left no discernible traces . . . which demands an arbitrary choice, not subject to any verification.

Facing Too Large
an Expanse

To be forced into a confrontation with nature. For example, to find oneself in the mountain forests somewhere along the Feather River, unprotected among the boulders, the five-foot-thick trunks of pines, the maze of dry, parched earth. We are usually protected, to some degree, by the praise and condemnation we portion out, by the part we take in exchanging boasts and deceptions, by clinging to one another—the scientist concentrates on other scientists, the printer on other printers, the artist on other artists, the politician on other politicians. All this makes for a cocoon of constantly renewed dependencies, which infuses time with value—progress, regression, evolution, revolution, a revolution in the preparation of dyes, topless bathing suits. The deeper we immerse ourselves in that cocoon woven of speech, pictures moving on screens, paper spat out of rotary presses, the safer we are. But the consistency of that cocoon varies and is different from one country to the next. I do not wish to play games with chains of causes and effects, and so will simply acknowledge that this continent possesses something like a spirit which malevolently undoes any attempts to subdue it. The enormity of the violated but always victorious expanse, the undulant skin of the

9

earth diminishes our errors and merits. In the presence of the pines by the Feather River, or on rocky promontories spattered by the ocean's white explosions where the wind bears the barking of sea lions, or on the slopes of Mt. Tamalpais, where the border of ocean and land, shattered into promontories, looks like the first day of creation, I stand stripped and destitute. I have not achieved anything, I have taken no part in evolution or revolution, I can boast of nothing, for here the entire collective game of putting oneself above or beneath others falls apart. Strangeness, indifference, eternal stone, stone-like eternity, and compared to it, I am a split second of tissue, nerve, pumping heart, and, worst of all, I am subject to the same incomprehensible law ruling what is here before me, which I see only as self-contained and opposed to all meaning.

I do not number myself among those who seek unusual landscapes, nor do I take photographs of nature's panoramas. To itself neither beautiful nor ugly, nature no doubt is only a screen where people's inner hells and heavens are projected. But the majestic expanse of the Pacific seacoast has imperceptibly worked its way into my dreams, remaking me, stripping me down, and perhaps thereby liberating me. For a long time I cunningly forbade myself to encounter that chaos which dispenses with valuation; I tried not to overstep the limits of what is human and thus inclines one to predictions either hopeful or gloomy; I imposed discipline on myself—I devised work, commitments, always aware that I was only being evasive, postponing the moment when I must clash with what awaits me close at hand.

We spread papers on a table beneath a tree and try to write or add columns of figures; the uneasy leaves, stirred by the wind, the birds in flight, the drone of insects—that incommensurability between open space and the operations of the mind—immediately drive us to a place with four walls where our activities seem to acquire importance and dignity. Cocoons, caves, rooms, doors, enclosures, lairs, those underground galleries where Cro-Magnon man ventured, though endangered by cave-dwelling hyenas, so that in the farthest, deepest corner, he could draw magical beasts by torchlight: only there did his work become enormous, only from there could it govern the fate of the live animals on the surface of the earth.

Now I seek shelter in these pages, but my humanistic zeal has been weakened by the mountains and the ocean, by those many moments when I have gazed upon boundless immensities with a feeling akin to nausea, the wind ravaging my little homestead of hopes and intentions.

Symbolic Mountains
and Forests

Thus, in general, the garden corresponds to heavenly intelligence and wisdom; for that reason, heaven is called the garden of God and paradise is called by man heavenly paradise. Trees, according to their type, correspond to the perception and cognition of the good and the true from which intelligence and wisdom derive. For that reason, the ancients, proficient in the knowledge of correspondences, performed their sacred rituals in groves. And thus trees so often replace Scripture, and the sky the church, and thus man is likened to a grape-vine, an olive tree, a cedar and other trees, while good deeds are likened to fruits.

Emanuel Swedenborg, *Heaven and Its Wonders, and Hell*

How is it that nature seems to contain the shades of our feelings and passions, that its images can be serene, menacing, smiling, gloomy, benign, kind, mournful? I have read a good deal of Emanuel Swedenborg, the father of Symbolism in poetry. Like the majority of my contemporaries, I have, however, been deprived of faith in the pre-existence of material forms as ideas before they were clothed in flesh, or as the expression of certain spiritual states. For me an apple tree evokes many associations, because man has been fond of trees for ages and they have served his imagination in religion, poetry, and painting, not because the apple tree was destined for that use even before the creation of the world. The lion struck primitive hunters as a dangerous but splendid adversary, but probably no royal crown had been given him before human beings appeared in the lands where lions lived. A mountain peak has always been the proper place to contact the Divinity, but Sinai, Patmos, the monasteries built on the rocks, all corresponded to a need for rising above the confusion of daily endeavors, drawing nearer to the sky and making mortal men's short-lived troubles seem insignificant. Thus, before the liquid crust of the earth had begun to cool, mountains were not thought of as foundations for future temples or for opposed linguistic concepts such as baseness and loftiness.

Those are the reasonable explanations I offer myself, but experience, unschooled and stubborn, forces landscape obsessions and beast symbols upon me as if, within the forms perceived by the senses, there were a rich and hidden voice saying the same thing to everyone. Perhaps a memory older than our own lives, the memory of the species, circulates through us with our blood. That memory affirms our identity with others, and also makes us able to understand each other to some degree. All our metaphors revolve around sensations of above and below, darkness and light, greenery, fire, water; the same smile appears on every face at the sight of a bird, and the fear of touching a snake is common to us all.

There is nothing unusual in my rendering trees honor— people have been doing this since time immemorial, and the thrust of the trunk, from roots beneath the earth, through our middle dimension, to the sky, where the leaves sway, has always lent credence to the division of existence into three zones. Trees were writing their own Divine Comedy about the ascent from hell to the high spheres of heaven long before Dante wrote his. I wouldn't know how to dwell in a treeless country, and where I live now, the compass of my dreams always points north.

The redwood forest, the remains of a virgin sequoia forest. The interiors of certain Gothic cathedrals—Strasbourg, for example—replicate man's smallness and helplessness in his middle zone between hell and heaven, amid the columns of the primeval forests which still covered large areas of Europe when the cathedrals were built. But Europe never had trees like the redwoods, whose life spans number over two thousand years. This forest is the idea of forest, a prototype drawn by God; no church columns attain that height, and never does a church's semi-darkness contrast so sharply with a ray slanting in from above the reach of sight. Small human figures are diminished not by the redwoods' trunks, too huge for comparisons, but by a lower level, in relation to ferns larger than a man and to the fallen, moss-covered logs which sprout new green shoots. To confirm their value as a forest symbol: the redwoods are such that the chunk of a felled tree does not die but regenerates itself in a multitude of swiftly growing sprigs.

Crater Lake . . . Twenty-odd miles outlined by the impeccably straight line of the empty highway, whose incline is so gradual that only the strain of the motor reminds you of it, and on both sides of the lake, nothing but a forest of paltry dwarf pines on lava-strewn ground, the boredom so great the eyes become sticky with sleep. Then the road winds around the slopes of the mountain, its peak broken off by a volcanic eruption, and finally leads to a view of the lake in that crater ringed by stones. Its banks are steep, inaccessible, devoid of vegetation; the water is a horrifying color, a poison blue, too pure, too absolute. As if to stress that this geological caprice resists every use, there is also an inaccessible island, a stone pyramid breaking the uniformity of the lake's surface. Rationally speaking, there is insufficient data to assume that anyone finding himself in this landscape will also read it as a code of pure sterility. Nevertheless, this excessive splendor seems to conceal some idea, and perhaps even the bed of the highway traced among the dwarf pines had been readied long ago in anticipation that someone would drive along it, someone who would grasp the intentions of its hidden, perverse Creator.

Or again, in the south, Death Valley. It's obvious what it is: the dried-out bottom of a great salt lake, a desert with an almost kiln-like temperature, a depression significantly beneath sea level. Yes, but the name given it corresponds to its essence—everyone's idea of the Valley of Jehoshaphat. A silence so mighty it reverberates with the shifting sands in the dunes, the crunch of the petrified salt underfoot, a sky without clouds or circling birds, the horizon closed in on all sides by mountain ranges the color of their own mineral deposits—verdigris, an aggressive gall, a dreary red with a touch of "bull's blood." Then it begins to seem that throughout our lives we have been striving to get here, to this place where our most vivid memories fade, the weaker ones lose their consistency entirely and go to pieces; it costs us great effort to reinstate their significance, continuity breaks, scenes unconnected with anything else arise in our minds— the tango danced by the crowd at a student ball in a distant epoch, for example, as if the phantasmagorical quality of those dancers were appropriate to this desert which turns the living into phantoms.

Animals. The enigmatic quality of our relationship to the bear—fond affection mixed with fear, the ancient tribal ritual of apologizing after killing one, children's furry teddy bears. Our playful liking for raccoons, those thieves raiding forest campgrounds, cunning creatures able to open nearly any sort of food container with their paws. A sort of anxiety upon seeing caterpillars or worms swarming on a stump or a piece of meat, and the same cylindrical shapes, the same blind squirmings of sea lions on a block of basalt jutting out of the sea. Binoculars reveal the mighty bodies of the males amid their harems, their wrinkled muzzles open in roars of warning, they roll over each other, they battle, the young play, pushing each other off the surf-washed slabs into the boiling foam. In spite of myself, unable to satisfy myself with the statement that this simply is, I ask—what does this mean? Is it an allusion to the similarity of micro and macro movements, the uncertain attempts at spatial orientation common to microbes and worms and those sea lions, as well, whose way of life, after all, is the result of limbs unadapted to moving on land? Is this some signal informing us that more elements than the air of birds and men are inhabitable, since those warm-blooded relations of ours can feel at home in the dark ocean where life is cold? Is there some significance here I am unaware of? Or no significance at all?

Remembrance of
a Certain Love

When I was a boy, I was quite curious about things that
ran, flew, and crept, things that grew, things that could be
watched and touched, and I had no interest in words. I
devoured books, but I saw them as information about actual events and adventures, and if I came across some "self-
sufficient" words (though I would not have been able to
call them that then), descriptions of feelings or landscapes,
I thought them stupid and skipped the page. Every so often,
a volume of poetry would end up in my hands and would at
once repel me with its falseness. The same falseness perme-
ated the bows, smiles, and empty chitchat exchanged by
adults, which was ridiculous because they thought no one
would ever notice that it was all only make-believe.

Still, in another way, I was an admirer of words, though
not of those formed into phrases and sentences. A natural-
ist, I collected May bugs asphyxiated by formalin fumes
and impaled on pins, plant specimens in herbariums, bird
eggs gathered in thickets at the cost of scrapes on my face
and bare feet; I was certain of the special importance of my
activity and I would have rejected as insulting any sugges-
tion that I was not alone among my peers in experiencing
such passion. I was a Romeo, and my Juliet was both the

boundless profusion of forms and colors and the one particular insect or bird holding me spellbound for whole days
or weeks. But I was falling so totally in love, let us
be properly suspicious, through an intermediary. What really fascinated me were the color illustrations in nature
books and atlases, not the Juliet of nature, but her portrait
rendered by draftsmen or photographers. I suffered no less
sincerely for that, a suffering caused by the excess which
could not be possessed; I was an unrequited romantic
lover, until I found the way to dispel that invasion of desires, to make the desired object mine—by naming it. I
made columns in thick notebooks and filled them with my
pedantic categories—family, species, genus—until the
names, the noun signifying the species and the adjective the
genus, became one with what they signified, so that *Em-
beriza citrinella* did not live in thickets but in an ideal space
outside of time. There was a furious Aristotelianism in that
will to catalogue; I was repeating the procedures of ordering the world around me, as if childhood, boyhood, and
youth did in fact correspond to the phases through which
humanity passes. Moreover, my passion had distinctly male
features, it expressed the male hunger for demarcations,
definitions, and concepts more powerful than reality, a
hunger which armed some with swords, cast others into
dungeons, and led the faithful on to holy wars.

That love had a sad end, as do many loves. Suddenly our
eyes seem cleansed by a potion that has undone the spell;
the unique person we elevated above all others begins to be
seen objectively, subordinate to the rules which operate
on all creatures with two arms and two legs. Suspicion,
critical reflection—what had been a sheaf of colors, an undifferentiated vibration of light instantly turns into a set of

characteristics and falls under the sway of statistics. And so, even my real birds became illustrations from an anatomical atlas covered by an illusion of lovely feathers, and the fragrance of flowers ceased to be extravagant gifts, becoming part of an impersonally calculated plan, examples of a universal law. My childhood, too, ended then. I threw my notebooks away, I demolished the paper castle where beauties had resided behind a lattice of words.

The practical consequence of my passions was an extensive vocabulary for the plants, animals, and birds of my native, northern land. My emigration from Europe, however, occurred when my attachment to names had long since forsaken me, and recognizing the kinship of American species with these other, European ones only made me think of my own life—its migration away from obdurate divisions and definitions to a harmony with the fluid and the undefined. But the truth is that I am always annoyed by that sort of musical motif played with new variations. I had known only one sort of pine, a pine tree was a pine tree, but here suddenly there was the sugar pine, the ponderosa pine, the Monterey pine, and so on—seventeen species, all told. Five species of spruce, six of fir—the largest, a rival in size to the sequoias, was not entirely a fir and, thus, its Latin name was neither *Picea* nor *Abies*, but *Pseudotsuga*. Several species each of cedar, larch, juniper. The oak, which I had believed to be simply an oak, always and everywhere eternal and indivisible in its oakness, had in America multiplied into something like sixteen species, ranging from those whose oakness was beyond question to others where it was so hazy that it was hard to tell right off whether they were laurels or oaks. Similar but dissimilar, the same but not identical, all this only leads to nonsensical thoughts,

19

but why not acknowledge them? For example, what force is at work here, what origin—a universal law, the essence of tree? And does it contain the principle, the essence of pine, oak? Oh, classifications! Do they exist only in the mind or, in spite of everything, outside the mind as well? Jays screech outside the window (if only they were *sójki*), but they are either California jays or Steller's jays, black on top, blue-breasted with a black crest—only the cries, the thievishness, the audacity are the same as that of their kinsmen thousands of miles away in my native land. What is jayness? The brevity of their life cycle and their repetition of it through the millennia, unaware that there exists something like "being a jay" or "being a Steller's jay," contains, I think, something amazing.

On the Effects of
the Natural Sciences

There is no such thing as "I and nature." The clothes I wear, the technological conveniences I use, the verified and the unverified scientific hypotheses I have been taught, are not mine but my century's, and at most, it is only a tinge of the individual which slips into one or another set of given, ready-made elements. I would like to trust my five senses, to encounter naked reality nakedly, but between me and what I see and touch there is a pane of glass—my conception of nature, imposed on me by the so-called state of knowledge, and the lessons of biology.

The omnipotence and majesty of God discernible in germination, flowering, fructification, in the marvelous endowments of the earth whose plants and animals were given to man's use; then, later, the unfathomable intellect of the Great Watchmaker able to foresee how each of billions upon billions of gears would function in the great mechanism; still later, Mother Nature's eternal ingenuity and inventiveness evoking fearful respect—I know these stages of progressive secularization, attempts to transfer causes that first resided "above" to "in," but, unfortunately, this has not made the *mysterium* one whit less *tremendum*. But this is neither my subject nor my tone—every "today" of human thought has its own intonation; were it otherwise, we would not be the slaves of style, we would strike upon ideas of brilliant simplicity instead of becoming entangled in the language of our sciences and arts, that jungle we ourselves have cultivated. And now the tone is not set nor the styles determined by meditations on the Highest Intelligence, but by the image of automatic, incessant Movement.

If temples are not erected to honor the theory of evolution, it is undoubtedly for the same reason that temples were not erected in the Middle Ages to honor the immortality of the soul; obvious truths, like 2 times 2 is 4, are not worshipped—churches, like laboratories at a later date, only designated the logical consequence of an initial premise accepted by everyone. Try to overthrow the authority of science in yourself and say: "It is not true that life arose in the sea and that one-celled organisms are the ancient ancestors of the fish, amphibians, birds, and mammals; no development from less to more complicated forms occurred, no transformation and gradual formation of species; ichthyosaurs and pterodactyls never existed—rather, God planted the fossilized bones which allow us to reconstruct the appearance of extinct animals, one of His tricks to lead us into error and further punish us for plucking the apple from the Tree of Knowledge; the anthropoid, which troubles theologians because it permits no line to be drawn signifying the animals' end and man's beginning, did not exist either; the earth was created all at once with its relics and ruins, resembling those parks built by eighteenth-century aristocrats who placed fragments of 'Greek' columns at the turn of a tree-lined path."

Movement: of galaxies, atoms, the parts of the atom, explosions, dislocations, transformation. We reacted with anger and offended dignity when it was learned that man, too, belongs to the chain of universal transformation—that "he is descended from the monkeys." A justified reaction to painful knowledge. Previously elevated above things, man now had to look at himself as a thing; his rank as a mammal began to gain ascendancy over his God-given autonomy, and morality and law had proven to be something he produces as a genus, just as beets produce sugar, or so it was said.

Remarkably, when man was thus naturalized, he showed an ever-greater tendency to humanize nature. The animals in medieval fabliaux speak and behave like people because they are people in animal guise, quite the opposite of animals in human guise, that principal obsession of modern writers. Pitying the animal in himself, his pain, fear, and dependence on physiological needs, man, degraded, has acquired sympathy for every living, suffering thing; he calls existence a concentration camp and finds it an argument against God.

Obviously, the struggle with Evil in the universe is an old one; the Manichaeans were among the first who refused to believe such a miserable world could issue from the hands of a God who was good—because God had to be purified, they held the world to be the work of a malevolent demiurge. Later there was an increase in theodicies, clever systems whose aims were to prove that God, in spite of everything, does not bear the responsibility for evil. Yet, never was the position of those who defend the idea of a hidden harmony more difficult, never was Manichaean ferocity more aggressive than when the nineteenth century observed that the suffering of living matter is the mainspring of its Movement and that the individual creature is

23

sacrificed in the name of a splendid and enormous transformation without purpose or goal. When our descendants seek to define our times, they will probably make use of the term "neo-Manichaeanism" to describe our characteristic resentment of evil Matter to which we desperately oppose value, but value no longer flowing from a divine source and now exclusively human, like a Baron Munchausen able to pull himself from the swamp by his own hair. Then, too, will all praise of the body and freedom in morality be revealed as shams and masks. For the fear of hell-fire has not vanished; hell (as with Mani's old disciples) has taken root in our very subjugation to and helplessness against the natural forces residing in us, which today are the domain of the biologist, doctor, psychiatrist.

These are not theoretical considerations for me. In the presence of nature, I am not "I"; I bear the stamp of my civilization, and as it does, I have a sense of dread and repugnance for the impersonal cruelty built into the structure of the universe. However, I do suspect that in humanizing pain—i.e., applying man's pain to everything alive—an error is committed: different from the earlier belief that animals were just living machines, but not a much better error nevertheless. Perhaps those creatures without consciousness bear no suffering in our sense of the word, and besides, there is very little chance that we will ever succeed in reproducing the sensations of nervous systems less developed than ours: a wasp cut in two with a knife, or, rather, the part of it separated from the thorax, will continue to sip honey; a beetle who has just lost a leg will continue scurrying down a path with undiminished energy. Why should I assume the role of accuser when I am projecting my own experience onto that which is Other, and

my would-be compassion conceals my fear for myself: for I know that at any moment I can be exposed to an ordeal like that of a moth burning in a candle flame, and not only that, I know with certainty that a more or less excruciating death agony awaits me.

One way or the other, I bear the stamp of civilization, and if I guard against using standards which are too human, the alien Other besieges me all the more and I can derive no law for myself from its laws. My contemporaries (strongly affected by Manichaeanism, and like it or not, I am one of them) have moved far from any doctrines espousing harmony with nature and the wise acceptance of its rhythms as a guide to behavior; paralyzed by the animal in themselves (once caged in by the Soul, Reason), they have sought the Spirit passionately, but since God has been withdrawing, losing his attributes, Spirit can now be only human, the sole maker of distinctions between good and evil, set in opposition to a universe which knows neither good nor evil. Though suspicious of what I have received from other people while living among them—listening to their lectures, submitting to their influences—I do discover in myself a deep-rooted conviction of aloneness, mine and man's, in the face of limitless space, in motion yet empty, from which no voice reaches down speaking a language I can feel and understand.

A Short Digression on Woman
as a Representative
of Nature

In any case, I am not speaking only of today but of the period more or less from the beginning of the last century until now, a period which, in time, will no doubt be viewed as a single chapter. So I am unable to ignore a certain remarkable grudge against human physiology that has been held throughout that time. It was not so long ago that Schopenhauer was widely read in Europe and the pain of existence was a set piece for poets. A marked predilection for that theme was displayed by very young people; for them, our subjection to instinct, the insidious will of life, was embodied by the mysteries of sex, the demonic power of woman. Their cries of despair, often unintentionally humorous, attested to the mutation undergone by the old medieval fear of Eve's tendency for alliances with the serpent, a fear which had coexisted for centuries perfectly well with popular bawdy jokes about women's bodies. Even though we find this metaphysical pathos (outdated by, let's say, 1900) somewhat amusing, we should not delude ourselves, for we still belong to the that same spiritual family, and a great number of works considered belles-lettres are, in essence, a retaliation against existence, a furious protest primarily served by writing both cheerless and obscene.

Unfortunately, our embarrassing boyhood constantly renews this pattern. And no matter how much we would like to avoid old-fashioned anti-feminism, moments of elementary revelation are not easily forgotten—the concave is not the same as the convex, a plowed field is not the same as the farmer who plows it. The little boy falls in love with nature, which reveals itself to him as many-colored, magical, spellbinding, and he falls in love with a woman, a little girl from the neighborhood and, who knows, perhaps so erotically, vegetally, birdishly, insectishly, that he would give her his herbals and his butterfly collection if she demanded them. But to enter adolescence means to enter fear, the fear of nature, the fear of woman, who is revealed as a representative and an ally of the implacable order of the world. Even the very division into two sexes contains something inexplicably arbitrary: why two and not five? But there are two and they result in a child, and they seem ready material to be transformed into the dogma of the Trinity and the dialectical triad. If it were only possible to give oneself, to trust and be trusted, lose yourself in the other. But how, if the other, like nature, is elusively alluring and, though it arouses the desire to be rid of consciousness, will not be possessed except by conscious violence? The heavenly valley—to plunge into it, to forget, but no, it is waiting for the hunter's spear, the plow, the grotesque act of the conqueror, who, when he aspires in his initial happiness to pass beyond thought and control, is not free to abandon either thought or control.

A glance through eyelashes, lasting no more than an instant, a second, but revealing another consciousness, expectant, in wait, almost concealed from itself—such glances opened Pandora's box to more than one young

27

man in his early youth. The sundew flower closes over the insect it has seized, an adder glides among the flowers, a hawk tears another hawk to pieces—the necessary, the irreversible—and who would ever have dreamed of communicating with nature other than through conquest, competition, the strong the winners, and the weak the losers? An adolescent among adults, among those more mature than he, feels unsure of himself, vulnerable, spurned, excluded; and in the evening, when they dance on the veranda, enveloped in a sticky erotic aura, he runs off to the lake, takes his boat and rows alone for hours in the night.

With offensive smirks, the adults stress their own superiority, and what they call "knowing life" means nothing more than initiation into the arcana of sexual technique. Finally, we become one of them, we reconcile ourselves, saying that's how it goes. The indifference which survival requires blunts our anger at the common run of things. Sooner or later the fear of woman also disappears, though certainly not for everyone. Many people remain faithful to the wounded, ungainly adolescent in themselves and, in their heart of hearts, admit the justice of his comical, impossible demands.

Happy love, mutual warmth, mutual sincerity, mutual trust. But is not triumphal male force the basis of that union? The sinewy prowess of the plowman tilling the Heavenly Valley? That does not suffice (for, if it did, then human relations would indeed be too simple), but can love live on itself for very long without it? And does not the adolescent in us, while envying us, smile with bitterness too—he who would wish to be loved for himself alone and not for manly biological exterior attributes which are either granted or denied by chance? Does he not long for a

brotherhood of pure spirits, for the sword placed in the bed between Tristan and Isolde?

Nature. If it were only possible to position it outside ourselves, a background against which to play out our tragicomedies. Unfortunately, it reaches our most intimate places, and if someone admits to having an old quarrel to pick with it, he should, at least, merit some tolerance.

Religion and Space

. . . a blasphemous identification of space with infinity.

Since all our ideas have their origin in our idea of place, a psychology not based on an analysis of our conceptions of the physical universe must be subjective and erroneous.

O. V. de L. Milosz, *Les Arcanes*

It is worth studying philosophical systems in order to dismiss them; not they, but the imagination, concerns me. My imagination is not like that of someone who lived when Thomas Aquinas's world view was reflected in Dante's symbols, though its fundamental need—to reduce everything to spatial relations—is the same. Space, however, has undergone certain disturbances. To begin where I am: the earth, instead of being a stable, solid foundation, slips out from beneath my feet, and were I, by some miraculous dispensation, suspended above it, liberated from gravity, other regions, other landscapes would move past beneath me. Moreover, they already do so in my imagination, for, though I know it to be absurd, I choose to be an incorporeal onlooker, outside the system, in front of a screen on which the planet revolves. In so doing, I lose the possibility of dividing things into "above" and "below." Drawing a vertical line above me, I will not reach the boundary where the world ends and heaven's spheres begin to circle the throne of God. Neither will any plumb line allow me to bore deeply enough through the geological strata to come upon the caverns of hell. A seething infinity surrounds me on every side and eludes the powers of my mind.

There has been considerable reflection on the origins of the phenomenon known as individualism, on Byronic despair—the revolt of the individual who considers himself the center of all things, and their sole judge. No doubt, it was the contents of the imagination itself which forced this to happen, as soon as hierarchical space began to somersault. Anyone who looks into himself can reproduce the course of the crisis. The imagination will not tolerate dispersal and chaos, without maintaining one Place to which all others are related, and, when confronted with an infinity of relationships, always relative only to each other, it seizes upon its sole support, the ego. So why not think of myself as an ideal, incorporeal observer suspended above the turning earth?

Unfortunately, it was difficult to preserve the ego's lofty privileges. The "I" saw the earth as one of a multitude of bits and pieces in space and saw itself on that earth as one of a multitude of organisms subject to the law of transformation; that is, it became something outside its own self. A monstrous doubleness, a monstrous contradiction, enough to justify the complaints of tender souls. What is worse, time, always strongly spatial, has increased its spatiality; it has stretched infinitely back out behind us, infinitely forward into the future toward which our faces are turned. When Dante was alive, neither nature nor (secular) history, stabilized and recurrent, gave occasion for any such anxieties. Today I cannot deny that in the background of all my thinking there is the image of the "chain of development"—of gaseous nebulae condensing into liquids and solid bodies, a molecule of life-begetting acid, species, civilizations succeeding each other in turn, segment added to segment, on a scale which reduces me to a particle. I do not like this and I would prefer that chain to be another human fiction, because the resultant compulsion to renounce my faith in my five senses corrupts me, Adam.

Perhaps only our Romantic ancestors experienced the crisis in their imagination acutely; later there was a gradual effort to forget it, for some sort of futility, the futility of too far-reaching inquiries, seemed to result from it; better to return to human affairs, life among people. But after all, here, by San Francisco Bay, people gather at least once a week and praise God in Episcopalian, Baptist, Congregationalist, and Catholic churches, and in synagogues, and for all America, religion is what religion must certainly be in a land of human aloneness—I, Nature, and God. And it would truly be frivolous to try to evade questions which belong to everyone, though most people are ashamed to ask themselves those questions. They have experienced the collapse of hierarchical space, and when they fold their hands and lift up their eyes, "up" no longer exists. Let no one say that religion can manage without such primitive directions to orient people. Not the theologians' dogma, but human images of the universe, have determined the vigor of religions. The Descent of God and the Ascension are two of the spatial poles without which religion becomes pure spirituality devoid of any toehold in reality, a situation not to man's measure. One of the Soviet astronauts said in an

interview that he had flown very high but had not seen God
anywhere. It is not clear whether one should smile at this or
not, for those who kneel and raise up their eyes differ from
the astronaut only in that they would wish to shift the
spheres of heaven further away—a billion light-years away,
to where the universe ends—but they are unable to carry
out that operation; their faith is a struggle between an instant of intuition and an hour of indifference or weariness.

What could be more fascinating than to look into their
minds at that struggle between the desire to believe and the
inability to, as when you have almost caught a butterfly but
end up with a handful of air. I do not understand why we
have allowed ourselves to be cowed by fashion and have
relinquished important fundamental inquiries so that only
churchmen, intimidated and constrained by their defenses,
will at times admit to their religious troubles.

I am not afraid to say that a devout and God-fearing
man is superior as a human specimen to a restless mocker
who is glad to style himself an "intellectual," proud of his
cleverness in using ideas which he claims as his own though
he acquired them in a pawnshop in exchange for simplicity
of heart. Besides, it seems to me that we are born either
pious or impious, and I would be glad were I able to number myself among the former. Piety has no need of defi-
nition—either it is there or it is not. It persists independently of the division of people into believers and atheists,
an illusory division today, since faith is undermined by disbelief in faith, and disbelief by disbelief in itself. The
sacred exists and is stronger than all our rebellions—the
bread on the table, the rough tree trunk which *is*, the depths
of "being" I can intuit in the letter opener lying in front of
me, entirely steeped and established in its "being." My

piety would shame me if it meant that I possessed something others did not. Mine, however, is a piety without a home; it survives the obsessive, annihilating image of universal disjointedness and, fortunately, allows me no safe superiority.

Religion and space: but now the old is meeting with the new. The old; that is, space conceived by the imagination as an infinitely extended, all-embracing body in which the chunks of manifold worlds are stuck like raisins in a cake. The new means space-creating movement, for, since space is relative and not absolute, why would we ascribe to it the features of a cake or an elephant and be amazed by its grandeur? And here Movement, the destroyer of hierarchy, reveals talents which its enemies, who defend the hierarchy at any cost, never suspected. In his romantic frock coat, standing on a mountaintop, the solitary admirer of his own ego succumbed to panic when faced with his own insignificance beneath the stars. But would that reaction be appropriate now when "the greater" and "the lesser" are losing meaning, subverted by relativity? Movement causes dematerialization and infamous matter, burden of burdens to the faithful, thins into light and whirls into the original *"Fiat lux"* as in the works of those medieval philosophers who interpreted the creation of the world as the transmutation (*transmutatio*) of non-physical, divine light into light which today we would call physical. But the more time became spatialized in the imagination, the faster it produced its contradiction, "meta-time." In spite of the theologians' warnings, eternity always assumed the guise of infinite extension; only the relativity of multiple equivalent times has revealed a new dimension which does not possess extension or the other features we had ascribed to space. Only then could we imagine all events and actions from all times persisting simultaneously, an enormous conglomeration (another clumsy spatial metaphor) of film frames.

In the opinion of certain Protestant writers, the "death of God" touched the root of all America's religions, leaving them vital only in the realm of morals and customs. The ravenous insect eating out the heart of religious faith is certainly more than a textbook model of the universe, and it is not enough to part company with Newton to find the universal reference point. Nevertheless, when here at night in these hills, near the brightly illuminated atomic laboratory where experiments beyond my understanding are conducted, I analyze my imagination, I realize that it is no longer entirely of the nineteenth century and that, in any case, I have been freed from an image of space as a solid body and container.

A Certain Illness
Difficult to Name

No gypsy woman predicted that I would leave my native land forever. The people I now live among could never guess that I come from a place without automobiles, bathrooms, or telephones, that on our roads, dusty in summer, muddy in spring and fall, five miles was a considerable distance, and people managed without doctors, trusting instead to home remedies, charms, and spells. The scope of the cataclysms destroying traditional ways of life, driving people from their homes, has already been assimilated and is now taken for granted, but it still makes me dizzy from time to time. California is not the same to me as it is for the majority of its residents, immigrants from other parts of North America. I am still that same small boy who on his first visit to the big city was alarmed by the sound of water in the toilet bowl, thinking that he had broken that unfamiliar device by pulling the chain. Any car I drive is still the suspiciously apocalyptic beast which had been tamed by the only man in our district to own one, Count Zabiello.

However, my acceptance of California civilization and my ambiguous reaction—something like a shrug of the shoulders—to the mention of Europe is not due to any childish awe of technology. In the course of a few hours, an

airplane can carry me from San Francisco to prosperous
Western Europe, now amusing itself with the very latest in
technological gadgets. In what I dismiss with heavy
silence ("Yes, yes, but . . ."), there is as much recognition
of necessity as there is in all those who were compelled to
flee Europe, like it or not. It is true that I was not one of a
mass of barefoot illiterates locked for weeks in steerage
while crossing the ocean. As a statistic I belong to the new,
later wave of migrations, the so-called immigration of talents, which was caused by European stinginess. All the
same, I respect necessity, which is the same for me as for an
illiterate peasant. But there is something else that steals into
my silences. Perhaps a prototype is more interesting than
copies, and strong alcohol, at least in many people's opinion, tastes better straight than diluted with water. Con-
templations of the twentieth century do not incline one to
cheerful evaluations, but since it cannot be avoided, the
confrontation should perhaps occur where this century at-
tains its full insanity. I consider it a privilege to participate
in America, just as once, in the cities devastated by the
totalitarian plague, I thought that, if I survived, I would be
richer with the knowledge whose absence impairs the education of my contemporaries, and makes them rely on
rhetoric.

And my European friends, with their anger at America,
citing the charms of the old continent? I am plainly an
incurable European, and I understand what they are talk-
ing about. No one will ever succeed in defining happiness,
but certainly one of its conditions is that a certain modest
human scale not be overstepped. Happiness is also a host of
small impressions which strike us, though we spare them no
attention—the buttresses of a castle, a tree, sand, a dishev-

eled woman selling vegetables. Try this experiment: on your way to work, take a route that runs by large buildings one time, and another time, take one through a noisy marketplace like the rue St.-Jacques in Paris. The same ten minutes will either be sterile or life-giving. Is there anything exceptional in my need for a sensory connection with details? The streets of Paris have given me much happiness, as have the valleys and hills of the French provinces, where a slate roof in a cluster of green, a field, a footbridge, a grove, almost burst with the density of their unique, particular existence, every kilometer abounding with things to see and touch. This is not the same as zooming down three hundred miles of California freeways situated amid menacing, monstrous vistas, the light lurid on the bare mountains. There is nothing equally exalted, equally grandiose in Europe; its wildest panoramas are small and tame by comparison. However, I remember that the longing for wild, romantic landscapes was the creation of an artistic and literary fashion; people were not intoxicated by them when their fields were surrounded by forests nearly untouched by the ax; on the contrary, it was a pacified, submissive nature that was venerated. A group of small human figures contrasting with a vast panorama is what still pleases us, even in the canvases of the masters most sensitive to nature's beauty. But when those figures are missing, when they are all only observers sitting in their cars? Europe's landscapes are a metaphor of its entire past—its byways, its emotional attachment to what is foolishly local, the slow build-up of towns and principalities into larger complexes. The abstract city and the abstract theater of nature, something one drives past, are the American metaphor. Everything is on the outside, and the airplane passenger may as well be watching television as the mountain chains, deserts, and cultivated plains pass by beneath him. The initial causes of the illness "ontological anemia," which torments the inhabitants of this country, should be sought in the lack of details in their lives from childhood on, a vacuum filled by prefabrications (for the automobile prefabricates what we see through the window). Among this illness's symptoms is the nothingness sucking from the center in, a sense of chronic hunger, the sort which occurs when an organism deprived of food begins to consume itself or, to put it another way, a sense of futility in striving for one's center, so one can never be sure if that center truly exists or is identical with oneself.

But, after all, European fastidiousness is of no use and only masks an irreversible process. The invigorating details of medieval towns slowly sink to the level of the curios found in the museums to which the tourists are directed by road signs. One may of course gush over Juliet's balcony in Verona, but to get there you have to pass through the other, real Verona, not all that different from a small town in Texas or California. The museum is not what counts. And a tourist from America hesitates at the boundary between the familiarly sterile and something not quite familiar, grimacing at this transition phase symbolized by the way Europeans behave behind the wheel of their cars (that phase will pass when Europeans cease to treat a useful object as their own private tank, a manifestation of their own personal power and ascendancy). The number of highways is also increasing, and more and more of the little streets where ordinary daily life once ran its course are now occupied by manufacturers of souvenirs and dubious works of art.

An irreversible process or, at the very least, nearly irreversible, and it is now joined by the illnesses already well-known in America or rather with the one illness that spawns the others. This is more than loneliness, for it also includes estrangement from oneself and those close to one. Let it be called alienation, though that misused word has ceased to have any meaning at all. Before this process is finished, there will be half measures, partial realizations, flights into rhetoric. If so, then it truly is a privilege to live in California and every day to drink the elixir of perfect alienation. For, even assuming that the human race is more resourceful than is generally supposed, it can begin to extricate itself from the traps it has itself constructed only when forced to by some ultimate affliction.

Migrations

At daybreak, the fog below is a stormy, swirling plain. The sun rises, the fog breaks, and the waters of the bay appear, the outlines of the islands and headlands, sheaves of sky-scrapers. Dew drips from the pines, hummingbirds can be heard whirring in the bushes by the window. The traffic on the roads and bridges increases, a glimmering multitude of microscopic points. Then I, too, join everyone rushing in pursuit of their goals and I become part of the great operation.

Footsteps, faces, gestures, words, aspirations and their fulfillment all seem miraculous to me, as they continue into yet another day. Perhaps for many people the smooth repetition of daily affairs is boringly normal, but not for me. My attitude is the result of various unhappy experiences. In my lifetime, states, social systems, civilizations, cities fell to pieces; for people caught in a cataclysm—and I happened to be one—the common things of life, once treated so lightly, are transformed in memory into precious lost treasures. Anything which allays life's inherent savagery seems fragile to me, constantly threatened by the chaos that I suspect is the normal state of things. Yet another day, well oiled, working well, what a marvel.

Whatever exists can be measured by how we desire it to be, but one can also make do with decent approximations. Man is afraid of pain, he flees physical suffering and hunger, and the cynicism which whispers to us that spiritual sufferings yield the foreground to primal needs is probably healthy. The idea of founding an ideal country, a New Jerusalem, brought the first Pilgrims to America, but its population is almost entirely composed of the descendants of fugitives who were driven out of their native countries by hard necessity. Suddenly, the improbable triumph of a premise unpleasant to people of the spirit—that the down-to-earth, the crude, the material, and the practical are stronger than anything residing in our minds; America is surrounded by the envy, admiration, and anger of the earth's inhabitants, who for the most part suffer from hunger or lawless governments.

The popular legend of America, so strong in Europe, does, however, beautify something which ought not to be beautified. Like every legend, it is kept strong and alive by what it chooses not to say; it selects only the attractive elements from a complex reality. People decided to leave their villages and little towns in the same spirit as a man considers suicide; they weighed everything, then went off into the unknown, but once there, they were seized by a despair unlike anything they had ever experienced in the old country. They were accustomed to earning their bread by the sweat of their brow, but their work had been incorporated into the rituals of a community with traditions, beliefs, and the blessings of neighbors. Death as a sanction, "He who doesn't work, doesn't eat," was a part of human fate, accepted in silence, but it was not inflicted on people as individuals—the yoke was borne by everyone together, family, relatives, friends. Now each of them was assessed as an individual, and, isolated among the isolated, they earned their living for a few paper dollars a day. They lived in slums, entire districts of the damned, food and clothing their only permissible goal. They came to know the fear of unemployment and a spiritual affliction they were unable to name, which they called nostalgia for their native district. Then they began to cling to one great dream—to go back. At the same time, however, pride would not allow them to admit their mistake, and they wrote lying letters home, reporting that they were doing splendidly. They knew there was no going back, and even those who, denying themselves everything, scraped together the money to return, knew in their heart of hearts that they were sustaining themselves on an illusion. Another, slightly more reasonable hope remained for them that, at some point, they would move from the district of the damned to one where healthy, secure families spent their days and nights in tidy little houses with white columns framing the entrance.

Resignation to the inevitable is the heroism of the common people. You can cry, rebel, but must is must, and so you seal yourself off and do what has to be done. Many of them did move to better neighborhoods, and some who had amassed fortunes to the best. The majority shifted their hopes onto their children, and it was only they who moved out of the slums and the factory housing. When affluence allowed millions to taste the good life, some memories still remained, though not historical ones—why should they care about the adventures of monarchs, battles over borders, revolutions won or lost? Here, by San Francisco Bay, nearly every man and woman who own a car and house treat their fate with a touch of disbelief. One man will remember long family deliberations in some corner of Europe over the impossibility of buying a pair of boots; or soup lines in the years of the Great Depression, when the only money coming into the house was brought by him, a child selling apples in the street. Or a woman lives with the memory of a dreary brick wall outside her window, a courtyard where a meager tree had to suffice for the forest she had never seen and had embellished with a child's imagination; or she recalls with sorrow the face of her immigrant grandfather, a simple man who never won the game, never acquired anything. For me the commonplace deserves to be praised, since history's volcanic malice rages beneath the thin layer we tread so carefully; for ordinary people, too, whatever their reasons, the successes won and confirmed each day are undermined by an element ready to erupt and return them to the helplessness and misery their fathers had to stand up to.

The Events in California

"Who knows, maybe this continent was not destined for the white man, and it might have been better to leave it alone," said a European friend to me. I would have agreed with his divining in those mountains and deserts the powerful presence of vengeful demons with whom only the Indians knew how to maintain alliances. But in California those demons seemed to evince no good will even to the Indians, allowing themselves to be placated only because the Indians remained on the lowest level of civilization, without agriculture or the use of metal. I am also always puzzled why the white man steered clear of California for so long, though word of it had reached him through the accounts of sailors. But, after all, those were unfavorable reports: a foggy ocean, parched cliffs, impenetrable forests, thorny brushwood. No one could have foreseen the citrus and orange plantations, the cultivated valleys irrigated artificially, the factories producing airplanes and rockets for interplanetary travel. In California, prehistory, millennia of generations passing without chronicle, leaving no other traces than the flint arrowheads found in the clay, collided with the nineteenth century—not the nineteenth century of revolutionaries and poets, but that other, rougher nineteenth century where every man had an equal right to lust for gold.

There was, however, a brief interlude. It is doubtful whether a great project for the organization of human society can be inferred from the teaching of St. Francis, but one Franciscan, Father Junípero Serra, born in Majorca, believed that he was faithful to the patron of his order. When he set out northward on muleback from Mexico in 1769, he was not guided by a desire to increase his own wealth or glory; he was probably not concerned about the interests of the crown of Spain either, although Spain, fearing the encroachments of the Russians on its nominal possessions, had a division of soldiers accompany him. Junípero wanted to save the souls of those who had never been reached by the Gospel. He was harsh to himself and his assistants and his eventual achievement would perhaps not have met with the full acceptance of the saint from Assisi, but it was the result of a deliberate plan that took into account the frailty of human nature, and especially the childish mentality of the Indians for whose salvation he was responsible. Baptized, taught farming and crafts, they were supposed to remain strangers to the greed for possessions. And so they tilled the soil together and placed the fruits of their labor in common storehouses from which every family received portions according to their need. Modesty in manners and dress, strict monogamy, participation in religious rites, and obedience to their superiors were obligatory, enforced by flogging for the slightest disobedience. Their earthly way thus mapped out, they could expect to spend the years allotted them by the Creator without great temptations. Neither were the arts to be neglected if they served the glory of God, and the more talented were trained in sculpture and painting; one example of their work is the interior of the Mission Church at Santa Barbara, where imitations of the marble dear to Spanish monks were hewn from wood by Indian artists.

Father Junípero's cell in the Carmel Mission has been preserved in its original state; his narrow makeshift bed beneath an iron crucifix is a touching sight—no larger than a board, it was there he allowed himself a few hours of sleep each night, no doubt deploring that he had to thus forbear the body. The gilded spines of the volumes in his library in the next cell I found even more of an inducement to silent meditation. Though Serra had wandered there from a Europe which, at that time, was reading Voltaire, he had remained indifferent to such impious, passing novelties. With the help of theological treatises, he intended to organize the little society he ruled so that it would be linked to the changeless, eternal order established by Providence. But the defeat of his enterprise was already being prepared in the domain he held in contempt, that of movement, light-minded slogans, and struggles. Europe had been infected by a kind of progress not to the liking of the great land-owners of Mexico, of which California was the most remote province. Aided by the Church (the greatest land-owner), they revolted against the King of Spain in 1821 and declared their independence; by that time, word of the extremely rich mission communal farms had long been circulating among them. So they grabbed the farms at once, scrambling for them among themselves, turning the small number of meek Indians who had not fled into farmhands. The great project had come to nothing, and, fortunately for him, Father Junípero had by that time been in his grave in the courtyard at the Carmel Mission for more than twenty years. He had left behind a dozen odd mission buildings made of stone and unfired brick, a road that linked them from south to north—the King's Highway, El Camino Real —and the name given to the hamlet by the bay initially mentioned in the chronicles of exploration as Yerba Buena. Until the Christians pointed out the inherent indecency of the body, the inhabitants of that region had walked about naked and dealt with the problem of the cold ocean mist in their own fashion—at night they smeared themselves with mud, which would crumble off in the heat of the day. In what later became the city of San Francisco, the impulse to bare oneself was to be the sole sign of fidelity to those spirits; other than that, the city had no concern for any of its heritage, least of all the precepts of voluntary poverty.

To undertake a project, as the word's derivation indicates, means to cast an idea out ahead of oneself so that it gains autonomy and is fulfilled not only by the efforts of its originator but, indeed, independently of him as well. Perhaps every project concerning human societies contains an element of self-sacrifice on behalf of those who will live after us. The triumph of California was, however, the result of crass appetites, the brazen arrogance of the ego not ashamed to proclaim that it cared only for itself; there is no hint of old Faust's dreams here. Taking a walk around the reconstruction of Fort Ross, not far from the mouth of the Russian River, I tried to imagine the ponderous Russians who once lived there settling around the samovar in the post commander's wooden house (so unlike anything American, it might have been brought from Siberia), or praying in their small wooden church. As to their diplomacy, the Russians did not make war on the Indians, whose realm began beyond the palisade, or try to convert them, preferring to carry on trade with them, but their cannons on that coast suggest that the outline of a project existed in their heads. In fact, the Russians had been drawn from Alaska to California by the abundance of seals and by a small animal whose coat was the most valuable of all, the sea otter; their ships were primarily instrumental in the near extermination of the still rare sea otter. At Fort Ross I indulged in historical fantasies, asking myself what would have happened if, on a certain December day on the military parade ground in St. Petersburg, the revolutionary officers had been victorious, not Tsar Nicholas I. In all Russia, the Decembrists alone seemed to have appreciated the role of overseas expansion and probably would not have abandoned the fort so easily. A dozen or so years later it was sold to the greatest landholder in those parts, Johann August Sutter, an adventurer from Basel, and sold without profit, for the convoy with the money from the transaction was ambushed. We may assume, for lack of evidence to the contrary, that Sutter was innocent.

Can Manifest Destiny, calling and compelling Americans to march west, as far as the shores of the Pacific, be termed a project? But they were on their way before that slogan was invented; fascinated by virgin nature, its endless potential, its promise, they were extending a flight which had already placed an ocean between them and their old countries. But here even the plural is deceptive, because each person was a separate case, every man played for his own stakes. Fenimore Cooper's *The Pathfinder*, with its internal contradictions: to move ever farther away, as long as it was farther from the constraints of civilization, into the primeval, the unnamed; but others would immediately begin advancing along the trail he had blazed, and once again he would have to curse what he had unwillingly brought about. Both Manifest Destiny and the war of conquest with Mexico, which put the entire Far West, including California, into American hands, were thus the consequences, the fruit, the sanctioning of an elemental urge, and not the realization of an intention established at the outset. Neither did anyone impose on those pushing west the idea of the extermination of the Indians as the highest, noblest task and mission. Passion drove them to it; the revulsion of the fair-skinned and fair-haired for the dark-skinned and the dark-haired was so strong it excluded the Indians from the ranks of the human, and a God-fearing patriarch mindful of the morality of his sons and daughters was proud to kill Indians, certain that he was ridding the earth of vermin. And many people were killed, not just Indians. Once again, the Christianity assimilated by the peoples of Europe had been revealed in all its relativity. Assuming that a Christian believes in hell, he ought rather to perish than risk his soul to eternal punishment only in order to eat, drink alcohol, and sleep with women for a laughably short spell on earth. So the image of hell was probably never able to supplant certain vague popular suspicions—that the image belonged to a ceremonial and highly necessary ritual that connected the members of a community in exaltation and dread, but was separate from daily labors and struggles, just as children's seriousness about games and their terror at fairy tales do not disturb the boundary between the real and the make-believe.

The wars—but they were wars only for the Indians defending themselves. For the white men they were police actions against criminals whose guilt was proven in advance because they hindered the immigrants in acting freely on territories that they, without hesitation, maintained belonged to no one. The conquest, in fact, preceded the project for conquest, and in their fervor the conquerors did not make much of a search for pretexts. The last independent Indian tribe in California, the Modoc, could no longer have been a threat to anyone in 1867. They were pursued, until, retreating higher and higher up rocky mountain ridges, they all took refuge with their women and children in a mountain fortress of caves. A siege ensued: rifles and cannons against bows and slings. But the Indians were remarkable bowmen, and it was only after several months that they succumbed to starvation. This could have served as a theme for an epic poem, but it will never be written, because the fall of that fortress signified the end of that tribe and its language.

Call it delusion, but a demonic presence can be felt on this continent whose apparent concern is that Christian man see his own nature revealed and that he unleash all his brutality. Something nameless is concerned with destroying ideology in him and, thus far, has rewarded him not for possessing ideology but for not possessing any. Despite all his Pharisaism, a person aware of all this tends to relate with a certain indifference to the violence men do each other. Complaining of the horrors of their own wars and totalitarian systems, Europeans can never understand this, for in their legends America is always only a picturesque adventure.

On That Century

Here the nineteenth century grabs at me from every side. This has nothing to do with architecture; California's cities are still encampments, it's just that the covered wagons and tents have been replaced by houses. Impermanent houses; their plaster gives them the deceptive appearance of stone walls, but they are made from wood, cheap on the West Coast, and more resistant to earthquakes. Houses are the target of California's mania for destroying and building anew, and there is some sort of elfish magic in the speed with which a small crew in brightly colored helmets raises the stick scaffolding and covers it with a roof. So it is a rarity to come upon a venerable monument, the brick edifice of a factory some seventy years old, or wooden façades like those in Westerns, with hitching posts. Only Father Junípero Serra's mission buildings are set apart by their permanence and distinguished patina; they were built around the time the king was being beheaded in France and hammers smashed the heads of saints on Romanesque portals. Not in architecture, but still the nineteenth century is felt as the only history here: in books about the gay nineties in San Francisco, famous for its bars and bordellos, in the days of the gold fever; in the antique stores with their collections of bottles dug up in the vicinity of what used to be lumber camps and gold-prospecting sites; in cemeteries on the sun-parched hills which contain the bodies of immigrants from Ireland, Italy, and Germany, who, for the most part, died violent deaths in the 1850's or 1860's; in the Wells Fargo bank's stagecoach routes; in the railroad tracks laid by Chinese coolies, who left behind a trail of names in places like China Camp and China Creek, or, here and there, a genuine Chinese temple that looks like the village churches of Poland.

I do not like the nineteenth century, with all its genius. Even when ensnared in the macabre events of my own time, both a spectator and an actor in the Grand Guignol, I always thought that I would not have wanted to live then and that I preferred what has befallen me. A century which produced words in quantities never seen before, it learned to use words to mask man's fundamental duality to an unprecedented degree. It is a human attribute to secrete what is called culture, just as a silkworm spins thread from itself; however, since every human being is also a body, his physiological functions make for a sort of endless jeer at the changing regulations of social intercourse and of mental conventions. I could be mistaken, but I sense in our more remote ancestors an instinctive, barely conscious leniency in regard to those odd arrangements. It was precisely their agreeing to the conventions that seems to attest that they accepted and employed them with a grain of salt. The loftiest flights were accompanied by a chorus, a chorus of crude belly laughs. Sermons, works of theology, sonnets, betrayed themselves by their own noble artificiality, for they coexisted with less dignified knowledge which was expressed through gross humor. The serene, carefree literature of the obscene ends with the eighteenth century—from then on, there will no longer be any genuine, hate-free pornography, which fact is only superficially of small significance.

The nineteenth century was a century of the spirit. A lofty tone was obligatory, and once that tone resounded, it gave rise to new, equally lofty tones that were in revolt against those who had first tuned the instrument. The spirit exploded the conventions, but whoever breaks conventions creates new ones in the very act—won amid storm and stress, then becoming absolute, too serious to allow skeptical smiles to degrade them. Worthy German professors in their nightcaps abandoned themselves to philosophical orgies. Poets tormented the flesh which imprisoned their boundless spirits. From their podiums, politicians orated about freedom, equality, and brotherhood. Ethereal pastoral duets were sung at the rectory; the peace of books and flowers by the window protected the island of poetic fantasies from the world. However, close by, in the industrial city, human phantoms reeled and fell to the streets from hunger. And that other humanity—down to earth, indifferent to the spirit, openly dualistic, for it reconciled its prayers with the primitive drives of hunger and sex— swarmed to the American continent, conquered it, and subjected California to its will. Those poor people who died from bullets or knives, whose gravestones I examine in the cemeteries near former prospecting sites, which, more often than not, were paid for by friends taking up a collection, knew absolutely nothing about Kant's commentators. They were driven there across thousands of miles of ocean or desert, or across even more thousands of miles in sea

voyages around Cape Horn, by a need neither intelligent
nor elegant.

Yes, it is true that it was the nineteenth century, out of
compassion for everyone like them, which succeeded in laying bare the dependence of the Ideal on whether the stomach was empty or full. The socialist communes and
phalansteries were to be asylums where nothing would im-
pede the blossoming of the Ideal, since the pressure of pri-
mary needs would disappear. Soon Marxism as well would
oppose matter to spirit, but that was a strange sort of matter indeed, matter as logos, begotten from the lofty tone of
philosophy. By some mysterious decree (that of Providence?), the spirit contained in matter had endowed it with
its own dialectical characteristics, so that matter should—
automatically, developing according to its own laws—lead
inevitably to the triumph of the good. The good, meaning
the abolition of private property, would certainly be
enough to cause the butterfly—angelic man devoted to sublime creative tasks—to emerge from the chrysalis of
duality.

California seems to me an illegitimate child, an illustra-
tion to a fairy tale about Johnny the Fool, or one of the
tricks history plays constantly in order to mark the distance
between the way it works and our ideas about it. The sky-
scrapers of San Francisco on the other side of the bay,
which I can see from my window if they are not covered by
low-lying clouds, grew out of an inferior element, a shameful one, matter not elevated to the heights of spirit. And the
California state flag, flown on holidays alongside the American flag, is a reminder of the state's idiotic beginnings. In
1846 a few Yankee adventurers, mostly ex-whalers who

had jumped ship, having drunk considerable wine in the little town of Sonoma, struck on the idea of proclaiming it an independent republic and so they arrested the Mexican mayor, who good-naturedly surrendered his pistol to them. Then they raised their own standard, a bear hastily painted on a petticoat donated by one of the wives.

On the Western

So many words, so much talk about spirit, but hasn't that cinematic myth accepted by all Europe, the Western, built around who is fastest on the draw, reduced some confidence in spirit? The Western is a product of California, and not only because Hollywood is located there. In the outdoor scenes it is easy to recognize the familiar grassy hills with their rocks and their black smudges of thorny oaks and juniper as either the Mohave Desert or the forests of the Sierra Nevada.

That aside, the annals in the old California newspapers can furnish all the plot lines your heart desires, for the art of humorous reportage was highly developed back then; in that regard, Mark Twain was not an exception. In the European city of my youth, one of my friends lost his job on the local newspaper because he wrote a verse account of the trial of a spurned rival who had murdered the bride at a peasant wedding. I still remember these words of the poet:

In her grave she lay, cold as a slice of herring.

This approach offended the editor, who saw it as a trifling with human emotions. No one set any such limits on the American reporters in the era of the lasso, pistol, and stagecoach, and so it is still enjoyable to read their brief, compact stories aloud over a glass of California wine on foggy evenings, thick logs burning in the fireplace. For example, the story about the feud between two little towns, and the pharmacist who was weighing powders when he spotted someone from the enemy town; tossing his powders aside, he grabbed his pistol and emptied it into the hated intruder, while the rest of the town did the same through their windows.

If, however, the journalist's pen filtered and reworked actual events in accordance with the requirements of humor and punch line, the Western itself passed entirely into fable, formalizing its own motifs, arranging them in nearly algebraic equations to divide the characters into the good and the bad, with the inevitable triumph of justice. Not having bypassed California in his cosmopolitan travels, Blaise Cendrars, the French poet, wrote a documentary story, "Gold, or the Marvelous History of General Johann August Sutter," which is sufficient indication of the distance between the facts and the Western fable drawn from them. Johann August Sutter was apparently neither particularly good nor evil, and his unusual adventures lack a happy ending. The bankrupt scion of an old paper-manufacturing firm in Basel, he fled to Paris, leaving his wife and children behind, then continued on to New York, where by means none too savory he acquired a little money and then traveled west. Reaching Oregon, he went on to Hawaii to organize a business dealing in slaves taken in the Polynesian islands. Later, after Sutter had prepared a consignment of natives who were to serve him as a work crew, a Russian sailing ship dropped him off alone (the transport of natives was to arrive separately) on a deserted shore, the

spot where San Francisco now stands. This occurred when
there were no white men in California except a few families
of Spanish cattle-breeders, a few dozen Mexican soldiers,
and a Russian fort with a garrison that outnumbered them.
Sutter acquired lands extending thousands of square miles
from the foot of the Sierras to the ocean, and he established
his own sovereign state, which, in memory of his native
land, he called New Helvetia, and of which he was sole master. His will caused aqueducts to be constructed, transforming deserts into cultivated fields and vineyards, and his
fortune grew yearly. A king surrounded by a bodyguard of
Yankee sailors who had jumped ship, he protected the Indians who worked for him, he waged war with recalcitrant
tribes, he had mule trains haul Europe's costly goods, including a Pleyel grand piano, across the continent for him.
After some time, his wealth fully established, he sent for his
family, the children already grown up; they came by ship
through the Straits of Magellan, for this was before the
Panama Canal. The French poet's imagination was struck
less by Sutter's scaling of the heights than by his sudden
downfall, resembling that, as he puts it, of Shakespeare's
kings. By chance, during the building of a mill, gold was
found on Sutter's lands, and it could not be kept secret.
New Helvetia was invaded by hordes that respected no
boundaries, hanged Sutter's Indians, plundered and pil-
laged. Soon Sutter had lost everything, and to crown his
misfortunes, his sons died tragically. What does it matter
that at one point he was paid the highest honors as the
founder of San Francisco, that he was given the honorary
title of general, that today streets bear his name and Sutter's Fort in Sacramento has been preserved as a historical
monument? In his old age, Johann August Sutter was only

a bankrupt man with a mania for litigation, appealing in Washington for the property rights legally granted him by Mexico, imploring congressmen for help, but to no avail.

The moral of the story is unclear, as is every line of fate. Though the French poet avoided the naïveté of the Western, he did construct his plot as the considerations of literary composition dictated. That biography could certainly have been presented ten different ways, and each with equal right to claim verisimilitude. Sutter was a cutthroat, a slave trader, an example of the highest courage and the energy able to realize dreams, an exploiter of Polynesians and Indians, their patriarchal protector, a farmer, a civilizer, a frivolous deserter who left his family in poverty, a sensitive husband and father, a braggart, a madman— whatever you like.

The truth of that bygone California, of all America, is elusive, ambiguous, and it would be pointless to seek it in myths devised to keep us from being overly troubled by the disorder of the world. Besides the skillful shot, the hand barely leaving the hip, there is also the wound which might fester for weeks on end, the fever, the stink of the sweat-drenched body, the bed of filthy rags, the urine, the excrement, but this the Western never shows. One is not supposed to think past the colorful costumes to tormenting lice itch, feet rubbed bloody, all the misery of men's and women's bodies thrown together, trying to survive when the rules they had learned no longer counted for very much. The tangle of motivations behind fair play in someone or the lack of it must not be overly scrutinized. Since the white man acquired what he wanted in constant battle with other men, red and white, a fable idealizing ascendancy, praising the righteous and damning the unrighteous, had to adorn

the victors. I have often felt inclined to predict that someday a completely different sort of Western will appear in
America, a Western able to extract from the documents
and annals the unrelieved terror and strangeness of those
days. But I cannot be that sure, because the truth would
still be opposed by the age-old tastes of the listeners, readers, viewers, who long to identify with heroes. Besides, let's
be fair, those annals are full of heroism, for the most part
the heroism of nameless people.

Donner Pass seems ominous to me no matter how often I
pass through it on the way from California to Nevada,
despite the fact that the written testimonies are contradictory and I don't know how much truth there is in the lurid
saga forever associated with that place. In 1846 Donner
was leading a caravan of a dozen families from the East
and when he at last reached the pass it was too late, the
snow in the High Sierras prevented their descent into the
valley. After the supplies were exhausted and everything
fit to be eaten had been consumed, even pieces of leather,
their camp became the scene of events which we prefer not
to think about, because we lack the ultimate certainty that
we would not ever succumb to the temptation of cannibalism. The highest heroism of the few people who chose
death in an impossible attempt to cross the mountains and
bring help from the valley remains the irreducible secret of
their personal fate, just as it would later on for some behind
the barbed wire of European prisons.

I and They

You are not a historian, so why does the past preoccupy you, and why do you venerate ghosts more mute here in America than anywhere else? I care neither about placating them nor about being impartial. I am simply bringing certain of my mind's wishes to the surface, thereby revealing my particular sensibility that chooses one thing and omits another. That sensibility is not like that of Chateaubriand when he set the action of his *Atala* in the forests of America. There is nothing exotic left in the world, and the local ought not to conceal what is universally human. However, American exoticism, both the cowboy and the industrial varieties, endured for a long time, and it became customary to report on America as something on the periphery, changing but special. Unfortunately, the special case of exile and settling down in exile has now ceased to be a special case, an unexpected variant; it has become the norm, and what once passed as the norm now increasingly seems the exception.

My sweet ego is dear to me, as everyone's is, and it is only the implacability of time and death which truly overwhelms me. I am, however, immersed in humanity, subject to it, each day it creates me anew, with the result that my own scarcely felt essence eludes me. Since my raptures, frustrations, angers, reside here and nowhere else, since it is here that I judge and am judged by enemies and friends, nothing could be more obvious than to acknowledge that the humanity which surrounds me is a web of pressures and influences, the only possible object of my reflections, something which both submits and resists. Well then, has everything said thus far been moving toward yet another treatise on a certain society? I am not that naïve and send the old models left behind by traveling philosophers back where they belong. Their scope included sociology, anthropology, psychology, but those disciplines provide me no enjoyment, and though they permeate me as, directly or indirectly, they do everyone today, I have not found much use for them. And, at the risk of impertinence, I will say that, for me, they are the same as the cut of a dress, as a preference for one sort of earrings over another, as the colors in commercials and the formulas from which television's images are produced; they are part of the style and structure uniting the gestures of one's contemporaries, and had I a liking for the sciences, perhaps only a sociology which examines the self-confident social sciences would satisfy me. Fortunately, I do not, for I would then have used the garb of a scientific shaman to conceal my own preferences and biases. My own ordinariness makes me free, no one will reproach me for stupidity if that stupidity is plain to see and, moreover, not only is mine but has been imposed both on me and on others, a stupidity to which we have been driven.

To be alive among the living: what does science have to do with that! What is the meaning of such an inarticulate cry? However, meaning does exist, beyond the reach of all

reason in the meeting of eyes, hands, in the play of pro-
nouns—I-he, I-she, in identity and non-identity, in perpet-
ual regeneration, in the places ready and prepared, places
forever taken anew by children, the young, old women, in
happiness and unhappiness, in love and hate, a fluency of
becoming, a river. It is impossible not to mention the name
of Walt Whitman here, but not because Walt Whitman is
America. The truth contained in the ecstatic stammering
"to be alive among the living" exists separate and apart
from him, and even before I had read Whitman, his sense
of things compelled me to search for words and was the
source of all my curiosities and passions. The electric current of Whitman's *en masse* was certainly stronger in
America than anywhere else, and that bard, more complicated and more cunningly circuitous than is generally
thought, closed the conduits in himself that were too private and refractory and opened those favoring that great
current. When the poets of Europe were cursing the *cité
infernale*, populated like Hades with restless specters, Whitman extolled, glorified, and blessed the human element and
its irrepressible onward rush. His work has suffered a defeat because, though our experience of collective life is still
strong, it has now been seasoned with a bitterness which he
forbade himself. The young American poets turn to him,
the progenitor, the father of their line, crying: "Walt Whitman, come see what's become of your prophecy, your
hymn."

If you want to save yourself, detach yourself from the
world, throw a log on the fire and forget the dreamlike
illusion, for you alone are real. Yes, of course, I care about
the salvation of my soul. But neither the monastery, fast-
ing, asceticism, prayers, nor alcohol and marijuana will

protect me from what has now made its home in me; can anyone still be such a noble-minded fool to call this sense of things love for people when it is in fact dependence? This is not only the usual sort of dependence on the fortunes of a given community so that any catastrophe it suffers either destroys me or deprives me of water, gas, electricity, and relegates me to the era of cavemen. This is dependence on him, on her, for if they cannot be saved, then neither can I. Nothing at all to do with altruism. They are murky, a magma which presses on me, and hems me in, and exalted above their vain hopes and desires by my consciousness, I regard them with irony. Beetles moving their mandibles in thousands of restaurants and taverns, swarming over beaches, clinging together in pairs on the sand, then suddenly they age, stiffen, and die, their dry, chitinous casings are burned in crematoria or placed in the earth. However, I have lost the state of grace that allowed me to exclude myself from everyone else. If I looked on others as persons, precious persons, it would still be bearable. But I objectify them, I turn them into things, and no longer able to exclude myself, I turn myself into an object as well. But when I am with specific people, men, women, they disturb me as replicas and portraits of my own futility. This does not contradict the nearly cosmic experience of "being among the living," it's just that this experience is rarely joyful.

The Image
of the Beast

What sphinx of cement and aluminum bashed open their skulls
and ate up their brains and imagination?
Moloch! Solitude! Filth! Ugliness! Ashcans and unobtainable
dollars! Children screaming under the stairways! Boys
sobbing in armies! Old men weeping in the parks!
Moloch! Moloch! Nightmare of Moloch! Moloch the loveless!
Mental Moloch! Moloch the heavy judger of men!
Moloch the incomprehensible prison! Moloch the crossbone
soulless jailhouse and Congress of sorrows! Moloch whose
buildings are judgement! Moloch the vast stone of war!
Moloch the stunned governments!
Moloch whose mind is pure machinery! Moloch whose blood is
running money! Moloch whose fingers are ten armies!
Moloch whose breast is a cannibal dynamo! Moloch whose
ear is a smoking tomb!
Moloch whose eyes are a thousand blind windows! Moloch whose
skyscrapers stand in the long streets like endless Jehovahs!
Moloch whose factories dream and croak in the fog!
Moloch whose smokestacks and antennae crown the cities!
Moloch whose love is endless oil and stone! Moloch whose soul is
electricity and banks! Moloch whose poverty is the
specter of genius! Moloch whose fate is a cloud of sexless
hydrogen! Moloch whose name is the Mind!
Allen Ginsberg, "Howl"

Chanting his song, Whitman's turned inside out, Allen
Ginsberg was Everyman. The very body of a person,
whether he be educated or not, recoils from a cold, brilliant, perfectly consistent slab of metal, glass, concrete, or
synthetic materials which cannot be embraced by sight or
touch, and it recoils from the power residing behind that
armor, as well. Thus, a caterpillar adapted to the roughness
and porosity of plants is at a loss on the waxed hood of an
automobile; the grotesque efforts of a bee knocking against
a pane of glass indicate how ill prepared it is to meet with a
transparent obstacle resembling solidified air. A slab, wall,
or steamroller begins to move all by itself, its movement
unique, mathematically necessary, it looms larger and
larger—then you wake up in a cold sweat after a dream of
being crushed. Of course, seen from an airplane, this continent is desolate, the skin of an antediluvian beast, flaxen,
bluish, yellow, sometimes furry with forests; sometimes an
hour passes without proof that the land below is inhabited,
and only here and there does the mildew of cities thicken,
at night emanating a many-colored light, the gigantic neon
honeycomb of the three megalopolises of the East, the West,
and the Midwest. Of course, America has a dusting of
brushwood, green trees and lawns, wooden sheds, fences,
weeds swaying over rusted cars. But still the sign of Moloch
is everywhere and all the cities are one city, all the highways are one highway, all the stores one store, and to travel
a thousand miles becomes meaningless, for wherever you
turn, you come up against that same moving wall.

Why does a person tremble, recoil, withdraw into his
own fragile, threatened flesh? After all, what surrounds
him is his creation, his doing, he brought it into existence

out of himself, to serve as his own contradiction. But that isn't true—he, the individual, touching himself, the color of his eyes and hair appearing in the mirror, does not admit to a causal role, and he is right. It is not he who is responsible but that other in him who acts as a statistic; clutched by others and clutching to them, in the most human way, submitting to his needs and desires, he creates something which is inhuman, beyond the human, which turns against his needs and desires, eluding his control. There it stands before him, and though it would seem to be his, it is not, it is *on the outside*. It is no accident that I have spoken a great deal about nature. The greatest trick of this continent's demons, their leisurely vengeance, consists in surrendering nature, recognizing that it could not be defended; but in place of nature there arose that civilization which to its members appears to be Nature itself, endowed with nearly all the features of that other nature. It is just as alien and hostile to me, a single, tangible man, impenetrable in its opposition to meaning; it rules by its own laws, which are not the same as mine. The difference is that the old nature would offer itself temptingly, ready to submit. We were able to bore tunnels through mountains, irrigate dry plains, plant orchards and vineyards where buffalo and stags had grazed. The new nature, containing such great energy and achievements that forces greater than the individual have been compressed into it, casts me, you, everyone into impotence, evasion, a solitude with phonograph music and a fire in the fireplace.

To what degree one plus one plus one can influence that new, second nature and give it direction does not pertain here, because any semblance of a political treatise was ruled out in advance. Impotence resides not only in consciousness but, it can be said without exaggeration, deeper than consciousness. The higher the consciousness, the better it will comprehend the mutual meshings of the gears, the self-perpetuating mechanisms, and the clearer becomes the incommensurability between the channel once assigned to the turbulent stream and the stream which has spilled out of its former channel. Intellectual fashions, slogans, programs rallying people under one banner or another are weakened from within by their tacitly accepted transience. There has been a great deal of all that, but it was digested, broken down, and assimilated by the Behemoth with all the impassivity of a second nature, and the more it changed, the more it stayed the same. A lower consciousness trusts textbooks on civics, but they stop at arithmetic, at one plus one plus one, and pay no attention to the complex determinants concealed behind the arithmetic. However, just beneath the threshold of consciousness, there is a doubt, perhaps peasant in origin, of the possibility of any change —the constant conspiracy of the mighty somewhere behind the scenes seems to predetermine a social order as regular as the seasons. But this is naïve; the higher consciousness knows there is no such conspiracy, that function begets function for the sake of function, and what terrifies the higher consciousness is precisely this impersonal monolith, its glacier-like advance.

Weak, warm-blooded, what can a man do against it, not man as a concept, but the given individual? Never has the division between man as a unique creature and man as a cipher, the co-creator of the unintended, been so clear-cut, and perhaps it was the calling of America, Europe's illegitimate child, to compose a parable of universal significance.

What Is Mine?

Wise men in their bad hours have envied
The little people making merry like grasshoppers
In spots of sunlight, hardly thinking
Backward but never forward, and if they somehow
Take hold upon the future they do it
Half asleep, with the tools of generation
Foolishly reduplicating
Folly in thirty-year periods; they eat and laugh too,
Groan against labors, wars, and partings,
Dance, talk, dress and undress; wise men have pretended
the summer insects enviable . . .

Robinson Jeffers, "Wise Men in
Their Bad Hours"

My hair, my chest, my hand, and my life with its dates of
such importance to me. The only question is whether they
are really mine, if the hair, the chest, the hand are not
being generalized, whether the dates in my life do not lose
importance as soon as they designate points in a general
pattern. From all sides, I am besieged by television, magazines, films, billboards with incitements to health and happiness; how I should wash, eat, and dress is an object of

someone's concern, and it is myself I must see in the countless crotches advertising the slinkiest of slips, in the breasts
attired in the most alluring bras, in the musculature of
shoulders rubbed with the finest oil. If I were an ichthyo-
saur or some alien traveler from another planet, I would be
able to observe all this as a flickering of lines and colors,
but I am human, I have been challenged by endless appeals
that break me down into my components and reconstruct
me from numbered parts. I know the male and female body
so well, apart from any particulars or intimacies, that at the
beach or a swimming pool I am in a crowd of interchangeable buttocks, necks, thighs, and my every organ is interchangeable as well. I am weighed and measured, the
amount of calories suitable for me has been calculated; I
must accept the fact that my sweat stinks like everyone
else's, since everyone should rub deodorant under his arms;
bad breath is not only my affliction, for the young man and
woman on the screen who are pursing their lips to kiss turn
away from each other with a grimace of disgust, swallow
pills to combat their acid stomach, and then merge in bliss.
But the moments I spend in the bathroom are not spared
either, for the toilet paper calls out to me from the ads,
promising that it will kill all the bacteria which live in my
anus.

An anatomical atlas is constantly unfolding before me; a
hand with a pointer indicates the kidneys, the liver, the
heart, the genitals, and explains their functions. Whether I
wish it or not, I am initiated into the mysteries of the red
and white blood corpuscles, metabolism, ovulation, the
growth and atrophying of the cells. If my health begins to
fail, the white corridors of the clinic await me; efficient,

impersonal, indifferent girls in white will turn my naked body over, as if I were a manikin, hand me a glass tube to urinate in, place me behind an X-ray machine, take my blood for analysis.

But I am always naked, and not only as a physical object. My organs, those covered by skin and those by other organs, are naked, and so are the events which compose my biography. These events are divided into two categories—those that fulfilled the norms of childhood, adolescence, and maturity splendidly, and those in which something snagged and ripped in my relations with people, where "problems" arose. To me, those are private secrets, but I know I am mistaken, for all such problems have been catalogued and described, with copious examples, and not I but the consulting psychoanalyst possesses the key to them. Conversations with him afford me great relief, for I am made to feel myself singled out amid the universal leveling; my unique quality must matter. More than relief, this is an intense pleasure, for, after all, someone is immersing himself in the particulars of my fate, which to everyone else seems interchangeable, anonymous. Nevertheless, I realize that the point of the exercise is for me to understand—that is, to link causes and effects—so that my suffering self, which I now have seen as one object among others, is left behind.

I am surrounded by the dense substance of the collective, that opaque, obdurate, insistent other nature, but at least I have been allotted a zone in which I can move freely, care for my physical and mental health, enjoy the happiness of an organism working faultlessly, alive among the living. However, when I have to be my own refuge against the pressures of civilization, that world secreted by all of us, myself included, that other nature creeps up on me, constantly reminding me that my uniqueness is an illusion and that even here, in this circle of my own, I am reduced to a number.

On the Turmoil of
Many Religions

God is dead.

Nietzsche

Nietzsche is dead.

God

Inscription on a poster
in Berkeley, California

Only God can save me, because in ascending to him I rise
above myself, and my true essence is not in me but above
me. Like a spider I am climbing a thread, and that thread,
beyond any doubt mine alone, is fastened at the point I
came from and at the point where a Thou resides addressing me as Thou. What is called the rebirth of religion in
America is not subject to the rules that apply to pre-indus-
trial agricultural communities; neither would it be much
understood by those cheerless atheists, religious fanatics
turned inside out, who in so many countries oppress simple
people for wanting to teach their children to make the sign
of the cross. Besides, the ambiguity of the secondhand ideas
now in circulation is so great that their very chaos should
invite analysis; there are, however, obstacles, and such

analysis is rare, so, in keeping with my purpose, I am venturing into the unclear, where one can move only by blind feel.

God everywhere, like the products for daily hygiene and medications, God on the dollar, In God We Trust, the national God, guarantor of the established order, helping those who believe in him, multiplying their sheep and camels, or their machines, punishing non-believers, demanding a choice: either with him or against him, and favoring a division of people—we the decent, they the godless. The wealth of nations and individuals is the external proof of a proper relation to God, their obedience and virtue; poverty betrays an inner defect and attests to grave transgressions. By attending church, a person shows his neighbors he is trustworthy, for either he has grounds for being grateful to God or the very fact that he is there to partake of the ritual means that divine protection will spare him from ruin. Unfortunately, the substance of that God is withering away; his name, uttered from pulpits and public tribunals, is as empty as the names of the gods in the Roman Empire and serves only as a demonstration of loyalty to traditional values. This is, moreover, a God hated by an ever-increasing number of people. A God being turned into a laughing-stock, a retired Jove with old-fashioned ways, whose existence is taken literally by no one.

Religions are totalities with structures of their own, and they resist the changes occurring around them as a church tower on a square resists the vibrations caused by the rush of traffic. However, they are not completely protected from the movement which surrounds them and which gradually crumbles them. Just as the physical church has ceased to be the focal point of a city, so has the religious system once embracing philosophy, science, and art been cut off from those disciplines, and the new systems are ill-disposed to religion. The civilization in which I reside denies religion, but the preservation of appearances, the multitude of extremely well organized churches, and their financial power, keeps the situation opaque. Every day of my life, with its swarm of perceptions, trains me in anti-religion, and I am unable to find any intelligible purpose in gigantic neon signs proclaiming "Jesus saves" in a sinister landscape of concrete coils, crushed scrap iron in automobile graveyards, factories, peeling shacks. If people did not put all this here, then who did? It was done by people and yet not quite—people cut off from themselves, overtaken by the petrified excretions produced by their own interactions. I turn on the radio in the car and again am unable to connect man as an intelligent being with this gibberish of sermons, incitements, and incantations side by side with jazz and concrete music. Truly, the language speaks through them more than they speak the language, and this makes for the omnipotence of self-perpetuating form. All that remains is to trace the effects of my being exposed to a mass of symbols that allow for no coherent arrangement. This undermines my confidence, the common language is destroyed, and other people, with their own ways of behaving, have to be taken like species of animals, they simply *are*, and such tolerance makes the human world inert and passive, changes it into nature. Thus, I think of ancient Rome and it seems to me that the circle has closed, that I am a spectator at the time when the ground had already been prepared for Christianity, though now, in turn, Christianity is itself perhaps no more than one of many dying cults. It is the same now as in Rome when there had to have been a raging turmoil of competing gods, gods everyone knew to be hollow, mere figures of speech, and the more that knowledge spread, the more avidly were the purely linguistic ceremonial forms clutched at and used for mutual reassurance.

However, this is only a superficial argument, these categories are too general, something essential eludes them. I cannot usurp the secure position of the spectator for myself if, apart from all the conformism and adjustments, there is still any individual, man or woman, who partakes of religious worship. I cannot assume that in what they think and feel they are completely dissimilar from me. Every person is open, penetrable, unconsciously absorbing images created by science and technology, the smallest gadget contains a world view; at the same time, every person, by virtue of his or her humanity, has a profound need to worship, and the resultant contradiction is mine as well. I see nothing shameful in admitting that our desire to worship goes hand in hand with our concern for ourselves. That would be shameful only if human life were not what it is—a fundamental deprivation, an impossibility, a burden which cannot be borne but which is borne due to a mixture of blindness and heroism. I desire a God who would gaze upon me, who would increase my sheep and camels, who would love me and help me in misfortune, who would save me from the nothingness of death, to whom I could each day render homage and gratitude. God should have a beard and stroll the heavenly pastures. It is no accident that Swedenborg testifies to having met an especially large number of Africans in heaven, for they had imagined God naïvely, as a kindhearted old man. Only a Creator resembling man can make an exception of us here among the rocks, the waters, and other living organisms; only from his lips can a meaningful voice issue, only his ears can hear our words. Whatever concepts discouraged personifications of God—and, after all, St. Thomas Aquinas, disturbed by the inadequacy of our language, recommended reflecting only on what God is not—people arranged things so that the divine would not lose its accessibility, and they stubbornly returned to their statues and paintings, bestowing especial reverence on deities garbed as a man or a woman, Christ and Mary the Mother of God. Even the Jehovah of the Old Testament, with his whims and outbursts of rage, though invisible, veiled by the fire of the burning bush, was a real presence, a voice, a breath. The revolution in our image of the universe which began with Copernicus made it increasingly difficult to preserve the tangibility of the divine, though the sense of space, rooted in the popular imagination, did not lose its hierarchies all at once. Today that space (a delayed Newtonian space) is being imposed on everyone, making it difficult to use the One as a point of universal reference, even if that One were reduced to a luminous point. Besides, no First Cause will satisfy my longing for protection. Standing by a swimming pool, I watch the breeze knock a beetle into the water. Sparkling in the sun, the surface of the water ripples with the beetle's awkward movements; below—a transparent blue abyss reaching to the tiled bottom of the pool. I toss the beetle a small leaf, but instead of catching on to it, it waves its legs wildly, and the leaf floats away, repelled by the current made by the beetle itself. This depresses me, for I am wearing clothes and cannot save him; if I return here in a quarter of an hour, the beetle will be dead. Perhaps this is an allegory of my fate. Chance rules the inexpressible multitude of individual creatures, and even assuming that there

are higher creatures here beside me, as unknown to me as I
am to the beetle, and they have the impulse to take pity,
our meeting depends on chance, just as it did for the beetle
in the unused opportunity offered him through me. Since
the earth has lost its privileged position between heaven
and hell, since man has lost his as one of the elect, and
since everything is subject to the law of cold causality that
assumes the features of chance in relation to the individual's fate, there is not much hope that my end will be different from the beetle's. If the beetle is not immortal, then
the immortality of my soul seems a usurpation and offends
me.

Religion has its inexpressible sides, but its symbols must
constantly be revived in the imagination and take on the
juices of life. Depotentiated, the imagination circles around
the symbols, but it cannot enliven them and make them
part of my life as a person, which is all that matters. And
thus I feel my existence lacks sufficient reason; I am going
from nowhere to nowhere, which is not easy to endure.
Today the "turn to religion" probably is less social conformism than fear: let us react to the collapse of traditional
norms *as if* everything religion, the guardian of mystery,
teaches us were the truth. You suspend your judgment and
you sing along with the others in church, precisely because
you doubt your ability to unravel all those intricate questions. Only *I* have difficulties, only *my* mind remains empty
no matter how many times I try to extract something from
my imagination. The others here beside me have no such
difficulties. Though I will not admit it to myself, each of
them is thinking the same about me. And thus collective
belief accumulates from the disbelief of individuals.

But I, closed in the boundaries of my skin, destructible

and conscious of my destructibility, am a speaking creature; that is, I need a Thou to address, I cannot speak to
clouds and stones. Existing religions only partially satisfy
that longing as human as speech, or do not satisfy it at all.
And when that satisfaction is gone, an entire civilization is
suffused with an aura of religious expectation and quest.

On Catholicism

Raised in the Catholic religion, I am not indifferent to the remarkable successes of American Catholicism; I read its press, I take sides with certain of its well-known figures against certain others, and I am even perhaps a good parishioner. Or maybe not. The division of people into believers and non-believers has always made me somewhat uneasy, because it assumes a qualitative leap, a different substance for the "believer" and the "non-believer." I suspect, a few exceptions aside, that we are dealing with a decision here, a will to belief or disbelief, resting on considerations which, relative to the heart of the matter, are rather secondary, and that the imagination of those who attend Mass every Sunday is no different from that of those who never set foot inside a church. I would even push this further—the difficulty the imagination must overcome to return heat and life to religious symbols may itself be a significant factor in the triumphs of Catholicism, which does not favor private meditations, and demands, or has till now, obedience above all. Catholicism is safer, the decision does not properly concern one's faith but the submission to or the revolt against authority, responsibility is shifted and the faithful comply—they kneel, rise, kneel again, sing, take Communion, and all this is done ceremonially, in a state of detachment.

The warm, human presence of a God who took on flesh in order to experience our hunger and our pain, so we would not be doomed to strain our eyes upward but could be nourished by words spoken by lips like our own. And the God-man is not one of us in our moments of pride and glory, but he is one of us in misfortune, in slavery, and in the fear of death. The hour when he agreed to accept suffering conquers time; centuries of change and passing civilizations are insignificant, short-lived, and no wasteland of cement, glass, and metal will make man different from those men Christ addressed in Galilee. He still has the right to proclaim: "I am love." The son and beside him the Mother, the eternal mother, forever grieving over her child's suffering, the protectress, the intercessor; and thus, in the imagination, the dogma of the Trinity imperceptibly flows into another, unformulated dogma, the Trinity of the Father, Mother, and Son. The radiance of that Trinity confirms the community of the living and the dead, the communion of saints, dialogue, and intercession. In this way, a purely human space filled with the rays that dart from eye to eye, from hand to hand, and with voices in prayer and supplication is constructed alongside physical space. All humanity, past and present, is, in truth, a Church persisting outside ordinary space and time, a Church opposed to the necessity built into the universe. Catholicism is the most anthropocentric of religions, and in some sense, through its own excess of divine humanity, it resists the exact sciences which annihilate the individual, and thus, paradoxically, is less susceptible than other religions to the disintegrative influence of science and technology. In Catholicism, even heaven and earth, the Descent of God, and the Ascension are not like relations between worlds but like those between human forms.

At the same time, however, since the Catholic catechism, a fortress built on a crag, cannot be chipped away, what constitutes its strength is also its weakness. The mind receives advance warning that it should not venture outside the walls of the dogmas and the mysteries of faith, and should bow humbly to things which it does not cease to find absurd even when it denies its own nature. There is merit to that interdiction because Catholicism signifies a participation in a feast, the partaking of bread transformed into the actual body of Christ. A mind infected with rationalism trying to explain how a little flour and water could also be the body of God led Zwingli to the proposition that Christ's presence in the wafer was purely symbolic. For Protestantism, that was the beginning of the decline of faith in the Eucharist; that is, the beginning of the end of the sacral feast. But how many Catholics, when receiving Communion, fail to overcome their own doubts and resort to a symbolic interpretation, since their minds can neither surmount nor avoid the obstacle?

Not taking part in Sunday Mass is a mortal sin, and before receiving the Eucharist, one must be absolved of that and other mortal sins through confession. But the faithful cannot grasp the meaning of Original Sin, which is reduced by the catechisms to the breaking of a taboo, nor can they grasp the meaning of sin in general. Sin is now being broken down into clusters of psychological and sociological determinants, it is being universalized, changing into a sense of undifferentiated guilt, and it seems pointless to whisper one's transgressions against a set of numbered regulations through the confessional's grille; the psychoanalyst's confessional has already taught us that what is hurriedly recited to the priest will not be the truth, and that absolution is obtained by feigning regret, while one actually treats past transgressions as more or less inevitable.

In a moment of sincerity, nearly every Catholic would no doubt admit that he is unable to unite the separate points of doctrine. Thus, for example, the Credo does not demand belief in the immortality of the soul, only belief in the resurrection of the body and life eternal; that is something completely different from the astral travel of souls liberated from skeletons and flesh. But at the same time the imagination is required to deal with the mystery of eternal punishment for the evil so deeply rooted in some people that it refers us back to yet another mystery, that of predestination and freedom, and thus the resurrection of bodies is linked with eternal physical torment.

But couldn't someone who wished to understand what he believes commit an error? That would be a fair objection had not Catholicism labored for centuries to erect a magnificent intellectual structure *around* the dogmas, and had its theologians not formulated all man's problems wth his own existence into syllogisms. As soon as a worshipper on his church bench does not limit himself to mindless compliance, which is, in any case, impossible, he encroaches on the fields tilled and cultivated by theology, which does not at all mean that he had to read any theological works. The very intellectual structure which Catholicism demands emphasizes the obstacles the contemporary mind encounters there. Because this system, perfected in the thirteenth century (and far from renewal, no matter what anyone says), belongs to another layer of civilization, another *episteme*, and that once lucid architecture is now becoming less self-evident.

The training which a Catholic receives in childhood inclines him to respect mystery; life and death conceal their depths beneath layers of meaning. Mystery compels humble submission to an authority which derives its power from the will of God, but the mind wavers between resignation and the hope that there is some path that leads into the heart of the fortress. Were it not for that hope, there would be no stands with Catholic philosophical literature in paperback in the vestibules of American churches. I, however, assume that a religious man who brings home a volume of the *Summa Theologica*, and sits down with it for some serious reading, is making a decision not too different from the decision "to be religious." The ideas he encounters offer insurmountable resistance; they weary him, and it could be said that the sleep sealing his eyes marks the line between the promise and its defeat.

The *Summa Theologica* and California—that makes for a tasty juxtaposition. California, washed by the Pacific, opening onto the islands of Japan and the Ur-land of Asia, belongs to the continent—or perhaps it is a separate portion of the globe, for California is more than just a state in North America reached by winds from across the sea, from the Far East. A mecca for seekers of mystical unity, for consciousness-expanding drugs, ecstatic sects, publications devoted to Hinduism and Zen Buddhism, for prophets preaching wisdom borrowed from Tibetan monks; that is, the capital of everything that is turning against Western man's fondness for intellectual precision, dear to Thomas Aquinas and his secular successors, and now supposedly useless and pernicious. Is this the beginning of a great crisis? After all, the science and technology that California's prophets depend upon for food developed precisely at that point when both the scholastics and their opponents began from a common assumption postulating a harmony between the operations of the intellect and the workings of the world.

Carmel

CONTINENT'S END

At the equinox when the earth was veiled in a late rain,
*   wreathed with wet poppies, waiting spring,*
The ocean swelled for a far storm and beat its boundary,
*   the ground-swell shook the beds of granite.*

I gazing at the boundaries of granite and spray, the
*   established sea-marks, felt behind me*
Mountain and plain, the immense breadth of the continent,
*   before me the mass and doubled stretch of water.*

I said: You yoke the Aleutian seal-rocks with the lava and
*   coral sowings that flower the south,*
Over your flood the life that sought the sunrise faces ours
*   that has followed the evening star.*

The long migrations meet across you and it is nothing to
*   you, you have forgotten us, mother.*
You were much younger when we crawled out of the
*   womb and lay in the sun's eye on the tideline.*

It was long and long ago; we have grown proud since then
*   and you have grown bitter; life retains*
Your mobile soft unquiet strength; and envies hardness,
*   the insolent quietness of stone.*

The tides are in our veins, we still mirror the stars, life is
*   your child, but there is in me*

*Older and harder than life and more impartial, the eye that
    watched before there was an ocean.*

*That watched you fill your beds out of the condensation of
    thin vapor and watched you change them,*
*That saw you soft and violent wear your boundaries
    down, eat rock, shift places with the continents.*

*Mother, though my song's measure is like your surf-beat's
    ancient rhythm I never learned it of you.*
*Before there was any water there were tides of fire, both
    our tones flow from the older fountain.*

Robinson Jeffers

Not far from the steep coast of Big Sur, legendary as a
hermitage for hippie Buddhists, is the small town of Carmel
with its mission, the tomb of Father Junípero Serra, and
another monument as well—a little-remembered stone
house by the water, built by the poet Robinson Jeffers
when today's elegant tourist and vacation spot was only a
fishing settlement. In that house Jeffers wrote works dedi-
cated to the contention that nature, perfectly beautiful, perfectly cruel, and perfectly innocent, should be held in religious veneration, whereas the human species was a sick
excrescence, a contamination of the universal order, and
deserved only annihilation. One may suppose, however,
that both his withdrawal into seclusion (made possible by
income received from relatives in banking) and the direction his thoughts took were not without their connection to
World War I. The scorn shown mankind by the creator of
inhumanism stemmed from an excess of compassion, and
many of his poems attest to his having read the newspapers
with a sense of tragedy, wishing neither side victory. In his
mature years it was his fate to follow from his solitude the

massacres of the thirties and forties, and what issued then from his pen was laced with fury and sarcasm. To favor one side over another, when he thought them both equally criminal monsters tearing each other to pieces, was, in his eyes, a naïve submission to propaganda.

I began to visit Carmel little more than two years after his death. The cypress groves he planted to outlive his name had been cut down because, in expanding, the little town had absorbed that valuable property. Of the former wilderness there remained only the crash of the waves spraying against the rocks, but the hill where his house stands is separated from the sea by an asphalt road hissing with tires. The gulls danced in the wind as they always do, but a helicopter was flying above them, its rotor blades clacking. The too-fertile humanity which Jeffers predicted would suffocate on its own stinking excreta was now swarming in the deserts, on islands, and in the polar zones, and there was not much reason to believe that one could break free of its grasp.

We spent a long time walking around Jeffers's low gran-ite house. Two large dogs were lying on the grass by the fence, a face appeared for a moment at the window. The tower standing a bit off to one side struck me most. It was there, I thought, that Jeffers would often go to meditate and write, listening to the ocean breathe, trying in his own words to be true to that single, age-old rhythm. Not to digress, I later learned that he had built the tower for his wife, Oona, and so he must have only rarely worked there. The rough-hewn stones he fitted and joined made the build-ing formless, and that worked well. Why didn't he maintain the stone's inherent modesty all the way through? But no, he stylized a bay window, an early medieval arch; denying history, taking refuge from it by communing with the body of a material God, in spite of everything he may still have seen himself as one of his own barbarian ancestors on the cliffs of Scotland and Ireland. That permanent oddity half covered in ivy, that romantic monument raises various suspicions, even as far as Jeffers's poetry itself is concerned.

Who knows, he may have been just an aesthete. He needed to see himself as a being elevated above everything alive, contemplating vain passions and vain hopes, thereby rising above time as well. He seems to have been impressed at some point by tales of knights in their aeries, pirates in their lookouts by the sea. Even during my first visit to Carmel, I asked myself if I was like him, and, perhaps flattering myself, answered no. I was sufficiently like him to re-create his thoughts from within and to feel what had given rise to them. But I did not like my own regal soarings above the earth. That had been forced upon me and deserved to be called by its name, exile.

I also would have been unable to oppose eternal beauty to human chaos. The ocean, to him the fullest incarnation of harmony, was, I admit, horrifying for me. I even reproached Jeffers for his descriptive passages, too much those of the amateur painter who sets up his easel on a wild promontory. For me, the ocean was primarily an abyss where the nightmares located in the depths of hell by the medieval imagination came ceaselessly true, with endless variations. My kinship with the billions of monsters devouring each other was threatening because it reminded me who I was and their unconsciousness did not absolve me from sin.

Did Jeffers consider consciousness only an unforgivable flaw? For him the nebulae, the sun, the rocks, the sea, sharks, crabs, were parts of an organism without beginning or end which eternally renews itself and which he called God. For he was a religious writer, though not in the sense that his father, a Calvinist pastor, would have approved. Jeffers studied biology as a young man, and once having accepted the mathematical system of cause and effect, he dethroned the Jehovah who makes incomprehensible demands of his subjects, who appears in a burning bush and makes a covenant with one tribe. Personal relations with a deity who graciously promises people that by remaining obedient to his commands they will escape the fate of all the rest of creation were, to his mind, only proof of what lengths human insolence and arrogance could reach. But Jeffers was even less able to reconcile himself to the scandalous figure of Jesus, which caused his stern and pious father to weigh all the more painfully on him; in rising from the dead, Jesus had broken a link in an infinite chain, thus making it known that the chosen would be wrested from the power of cause and effect, a power identified with hell. This was close to the claims of the modern revolutionaries who proclaimed universal happiness, but always for tomorrow, and Jeffers could not bear them. His God was pure movement pursuing no direction. Universes arose and died out in Him, while He, indifferent to good and evil, maintained his round of eternal return, requiring nothing but praise for His continued existence.

This is very impressive even if Jeffers's attraction to piety and veneration was not unique among the anti-Christians of his time. He composed hymns of complete acceptance, and it is unclear whether he was more a stoic or the heir of his Calvinist father, who trembled before *Deus Terribilis*. Perhaps those were not hymns but psalms of penance. And it is because of his ardent bitterness that I acknowledge his superiority to his fellow citizens who sat down at the table, folded their hands in prayer, and said: "God is dead. Hurray! Let's eat!"

I have focused on his particular obsession. Whenever he wrote about people (usually dismal tales of fate, causing unbridled instincts to crush all the protagonists), they are reduced in size, tiny insects crawling along the piled furrows of the planet. He achieved that perspective by contrast with the background. Or, perhaps more important, his characters diminished as the action progressed, until finally the main hero, having committed murder, flees to the mountains, where his love, his hate, and the body with the knife in it now appeared ridiculous, inessential, pinpoints lost in infinity. What did that mean? Dimensions are a function of their distance from the eye. Like everyone else, Jeffers longed for a hierarchically ordered space divided into bottom, middle, and top, but an impersonal and immanent God could not serve as a keystone to a pyramid. Jeffers granted himself the superior position at the summit, he was a vulture, an eagle, the witness and judge of mortal men deserving of pity.

We used to walk the beach at Carmel fairly often, gathering pieces of wood, shells, and stones, smooth and pleasing to the touch. The cries of running children and the barking of their dogs vanished in the double roar of wind and surf. In the hollows shielded by the dunes, vacationers built fires, grilled frankfurters on sticks, took snapshots. Nearly all of them were unaware that Jeffers's house was nearby. Jeffers, if one overlooks a handful of admirers, has been almost completely forgotten. But, after all, whatever his faults, he was truly a great poet. Even in his own lifetime he did not have many readers, and before condemning his misanthropy, one must recall that he was neglected by people who placed great value on meat, alcohol, comfortable houses, and luxurious cars, and only tolerated words as if they were harmless hobbies. There was something paradoxical in my fascination with him; I was surprised that I, a newcomer from lands where everyone is burdened with history, where History is written with a capital H, was conducting a dialogue with his spirit though, had we met, we would not have been able to understand one another.

But I did conduct that dialogue. He was courageous, and so he broke through the spiderweb of invisible censorship as best he could, and compared with him, others were like dying flies utterly tangled in that web. They had lost the ability to be simple; they were afraid that if they called bread bread and wine wine they would be suspected of a lack of refinement, and the more caught they became in the perversions of their cultivation, the less sure they were of it. He bet everything, drew his own conclusions in voluntary isolation, making no attempt to please anyone, holding his own. Just as he appears, distinct, in photographs—the thin, proud face of a sailor, the narrow lips—Jeffers's work resembles nothing else produced in this century; it was not done for the cultural stock markets of the great capitals, and seemed intentionally to repel them by the violence of his tone, which is forgivable but only if the violence includes no preaching. His work is distorted, turn-of-the-century, tainted like that tower of his, but after all, he had to pay something too, like everyone else here. In contrast to the products of the jeweler's chisel to which we have become inadvertently accustomed, his work is striking in its simplicity, its roughness, but at the same time there was something sickly in his simplicity. The tasks he set himself no doubt exceeded his strength, and not his alone. In a time when no one knows what to believe in and what not to believe in, he studied himself and drew a distinct line expounding his image of God, the universe, and the human species, for which he foretold a quick finish. He understood the whole of his work as a new *De Rerum Natura*, and how could such ambition proceed without reversals?

I fumed at his naïveté and his errors, I saw him as an example of all the faults peculiar to prisoners, exiles, and hermits. But here in Carmel, where he had his body burned and his ashes strewn to the wind, his spirit, perhaps reincarnated in the gulls or pelicans flying over the beach in majestic formation, challenged me to wrestle and, through its courage, gave me courage.

To Robinson Jeffers

If you have not read the Slavic poets,
so much the better. There's nothing there
for a Scotch-Irish wanderer to seek. They lived in a
    childhood
prolonged from age to age. For them, the sun
was a farmer's ruddy face, the moon peeped through a
    cloud,
and the Milky Way gladdened them like a birch-lined road.
They longed for the kingdom which is always near,
always right at hand. Then, under apple trees,
angels in homespun linen will come parting the boughs,
and at the white kolkhoz tablecloth
cordiality and affection will feast (falling to the ground
    at times).

And you are from surf-rattled skerries. From the heaths
where, burying a warrior, they broke his bones
so he could not haunt the living. From the sea-night
which your forefathers pulled over themselves, without a
    word.
Above your head, no face, neither the sun's nor the moon's,
only the throbbing of galaxies, the immutable
violence of new beginnings, of new destruction.

All your life listening to the ocean. Black dinosaurs
wade where a purple zone of phosphorescent weeds
rises and falls on the waves as in a dream. And Agamemnon
sails the boiling deep to the steps of the palace
to have his blood gush onto marble. Till mankind passes
and the pure and stony earth is pounded by the ocean.

Thin-lipped, blue-eyed, without grace or hope,
before God the Terrible, body of the world.
Prayers are not heard. Basalt and granite.
Above them, a bird of prey. The only beauty.

What have I to do with you? From footpaths in the
    orchards,
from an untaught choir and shimmers of a monstrance,
from flower beds of rue, hills by the rivers, books
in which a zealous Lithuanian announced brotherhood,
    I come.
Oh, consolations of mortals, creeds futile!

And yet you did not know what I know. The earth teaches
more than does the nakedness of elements. No one with
    impunity
gives himself the eyes of a god. So brave, in a void,
you offered sacrifices to daemons; there were Wotan and
    Thor,
the screech of Erinyes in the air, the terror of dogs
when Hecate with her retinue of the dead draws near.

Better to carve suns and moons on the joints of crosses
as was done in my district. To birches and firs
give feminine names. To implore protection
against the mute and treacherous might
than to proclaim, as you did, an inhuman thing.

Sex Provided

Woman is in her right and even fulfills a sort of obligation when she takes pains to appear as a magical and supernatural creature.

Baudelaire

The satisfaction of hunger has first place in the hierarchy of human needs, and it is quite easy to understand why the sexual myth has arisen in the civilization which began producing surplus food like no other before it. Nevertheless, the exuberance and ubiquity of that myth are astonishing and can be evaluated only by first forcibly detaching oneself from that which surrounds us every day. At every moment I am exposed to its numerous ramifications; the printed word, magazine illustrations, film, television, the music from transistor radios, have all been drawn into its service. There is a certain automatic quality to all of this, for the consumer's attention and thus his money are most easily attracted by appealing to people's most common interests. Furthermore, the increasingly rapid growth of the media is subject to the law of action, which, after all, consists of nothing else but people pursuing one another—either to kill each other or to make love. If I use the word

97

"myth," it is because, with the increasingly larger doses of stimuli and enticements, there has arisen a set of beliefs which are instinctive in appearance only and which are, in reality, like all collective creations, "artificial."

It is not surprising that the body of a beautiful woman excites desire in me, but isn't it something else again when there are a thousand or ten thousand bodies, more or less naked, offering themselves to me, their faces fixed in ecstasy? What is the meaning of their throaty love calls, the nervous laughter reverberating from radios and records? That abundance forces me to defend myself with humor, smiling and indifferent as a pasha in his harem, and yet, in spite of my higher, detached self, I am aware of the leg, buttock, hip advertising a new film or a new cosmetic. Quantity changes into quality here, and a new quality of experience imperceptibly and painlessly leads one to philosophy. And that is the philosophy of the Islands of Happiness, where everything natural is without sin, an earthly paradise. Knowing others in their nakedness and known by them in mine, I take and am taken, an orgiastic identity unites us. Except that the Islands of Happiness, once discovered in Polynesia by sailors from the Puritan countries, have been conquered by the church of hygiene.

Public discussions about perfect and imperfect orgasm; equal rights to pleasure for men and women; the Pill, allowing women to give themselves to love without fear of pregnancy; an antipathy to temperance as contradicting the requirements of good health; virginity as a humorous indisposition which needs to be disposed of—these were not subjects for our ancestors. In *Brave New World* and other anti-utopias, sex, made universal and considered an ordinary physiological function, appears, not without reason, as a major cause of depersonalization. What generally escapes the attention of the authors of anti-utopias (which, in any case, are already realities) is the severance of myth from instinct. The existence of the gods and heroes of mythology was accepted on faith, although no one actually encountered them, and similarly, sex in itself, the act of fulfillment in its purest and most isolated form, exists only in magazine illustrations, in the promises of advertisements, on the screen. Sex of that sort changes me into an object, as does the knowledge of the proper functioning of the liver, which is the one, universal liver as represented in my body. Normality serves as a standard of measure and is applied to my representative liver. But, unfortunately, in the case of sex, normality is only imagined and desired. The majority of men and women encounter certain difficulties and complications in this area, though none of them is eager to admit it, hiding the sadness of hunchbacks in their souls. The sexual myth provides them images which assure them that the happiness of orgasmic union is easy to achieve. Flaubert's poor Madame Bovary wanted to find in life the same love she had found in romantic novels. The pattern has changed and romantic love has acquired the name of perfect orgasm, but now, sung, spoken, illustrated, it beckons everyone to dream.

Has nakedness ever been for people what it now is for us? This is an important and philosophical question. A woman undressing in a film made in 1919 removes clothes fashionable in 1919, she is not naked but uncovered by what she has removed, and more resembles a woman from the same period with her clothes on than a naked woman from the second half of the century. Similarly, nudes in Renaissance paintings are husked out of the dress of the epoch but still are, so to speak, enfolded in them, except that these garments are invisible. The body always bears a trace of the clothes which covered it—e.g., belts or stays—but, above all, the trace of the bearing, gestures, and postures imposed by the clothes commonly worn. What is most important here, however, is the constantly changing manner in which we see the body. Bodies are not seen by some abstract "human eye" but by a person belonging to the style of his times, with a constantly shifting sensitivity to certain shapes and lines, so that his admiration for the naked or clothed object—erotic or aesthetic—cannot be divided. Perhaps the "body in itself" is as much beyond our grasp as the "thing in itself."

And what if today's nakedness evokes not so much images of "undressedness" but another nakedness, that of masses of naked bodies? Masses of naked bodies do indeed appear in old paintings, which indicates that the collective dimension was not then alien to the imagination; but, more often than not, those were renderings of the tangled bodies of the damned falling into the abyss of hell. In daily life, painters did not have much occasion to see many naked human figures, and perhaps that is why they shifted such scenes into the hereafter. Large numbers of people were not found even at the baths and, moreover, were of the same sex. Or, if the sexes did mingle, it was only in baths protected against the gaze of intruders. Beaches, swimming pools, concentration camps—that is, places where people voluntarily or by force surrender to the mass—are another matter.

Such communal places play a double role; as a direct experience and as images from photographs, films, television. Moreover, the distance between directly experiencing "being in the mass" and getting information from the media is diminishing, whereas the ability of people to identify with Everyman is on the rise. That word, "Everyman," refers us back to the medieval morality play, though then it was a question of the adventure of the soul, either saved or damned. Physiological humanity clinging to itself resembles a sort of coral reef. It was not by chance that, when speaking of nakedness and sex, I made reference to the concentration camp: human corpses, legs spread, their private parts exposed to public view, this is what the prisoners were to the camp administrators who assigned them numbers. The sexual myth slowly, gradually standardizes and deprivatizes bodies, changing them into objects whose stock is apparently inexhaustible, no matter what plagues might afflict the species. Unfortunately, the acceptance of the freedom we are magnanimously offered is laced with hatred and this is not an age of jolly pornographers. From Eliot's "Sweeney Agonistes" we learn that on South Sea islands there is nothing but "birth, copulation, and death." But "birth, copulation, and death" belong to the condition of man in general, they are universal, impersonal, even antipersonal categories and do not have the consent of the individual, for the individual wants more, he wants to be immortal and unique. Were it otherwise, the Islands of Happiness would not have become symbols of sinister boredom.

The anti-utopias of our century (Zamyatin, Huxley, Orwell) depicted societies under total control where the absence of freedom is called freedom. In such societies, the rulers take care to supply the ruled with suitable diversions to prevent mental anxiety. Sexual games best fulfill that function. It is a credit to the intuition of the authors of those books that they depict Eros acting as a subversive force, which is no secret to the authorities: sex is anti-erotic and not only poses no threat but effectively prevents the appearance of the passions, which draw persons, not bodies, together and engage them both as flesh and as spirit. The hero enters upon a dangerous path when he is awakened by love. Only then is the slavery that was in disguise and accepted by everyone revealed to him as slavery.

On Censorship

The word "censorship" immediately provokes a hostile reaction, since traditionally it indicates the intention of the
authorities, whether clerical or secular, to curtail freedom.
The very essence of Western technological civilization is
incompatible with censorship, which presupposes an authority decreeing what should be allowed and what forbidden, whereas the West's entire adventure of discoveries and
inventions began with a revolt against authority. Any school-
book can furnish sufficient examples of censors making
fools of themselves, beginning with Galileo's persecutors
and ending with the judges who order literary works con-
fiscated for immorality, precisely those works which subse-
quently enter the classical canon of required school reading. Nevertheless, although parliamentary systems have
guaranteed freedom of scientific inquiry and the right to
proclaim political heresies, there have still been efforts in
our century to retain the concept of an offense against what
is called public morality. Such attempts, as we now see,
were doomed to defeat on account of the ever-greater intimidation of censors, who have been branded fools and
reactionaries. Of considerable importance here has been
the anxiety of the churches ready to make concessions pro-

vided they could maintain their new image as enlightened and progressive institutions. The citadel of so-called public morality fell when the first gap appeared in the wall— general agreement as to the inviolability of a work of art; i.e., that anything may be depicted in words, stone, line, or color if the goal is "artistic." Twenty years ago the works of Henry Miller were banned in America, today they can be bought in paperback. This one example is enough to illustrate the overall change.

Censorship, or the lack of it, seems to originate in a fundamental choice whose consequences cannot be imagined while that choice is being made. If, in certain cases, the freedom of the individual should be limited in the name of the common good, a very great good would justify very great limitation—which means the same as great power in the hands of those who are to judge what is good and what is bad for the community. If, however, that privilege is not conferred upon anyone, it becomes hard to deny that everyone is entitled to proclaim his own philosophy, even if it offers deep and fundamental reasons for counseling murder and cannibalism.

In Paris in 1934 the Surrealists published a collection of poetry in honor of an adolescent criminal, Violette Nozières, who had been sentenced in court to a correctional home for poisoning both her parents. The Surrealists, combining Freud with Marx, dreamed of a revolution that would overthrow private property as well as bourgeois morality and change everyone into a poet, i.e., a stenographer of his own unconscious. Violette's parents were bourgeois, they oppressed her, demanded she obey them, forbade her to spend the night away from home, and so on. She poisoned them, and thus proved that hers were the values of the free society of the future. She had committed "a revolutionary act." Although in the poems praising her action one can detect some reflection of the collective self-disgust quite widespread in the France of the thirties, the volume appeared in a small edition and its influence surely did not extend beyond the circles of artistic bohemia. It lost out in competition with another European book, published somewhat earlier but read by millions of people, which also prescribed a better arrangement for society, *Mein Kampf*.

France retained legislation against acts outraging public decency, hence the trials of publishing houses specializing in pornography. No one, however, disturbed publishers printing pornographic books in English, later to be smuggled into England, Canada, and the United States. As recently as ten years ago, I read the *Memoirs of Fanny Hill*, in the only edition then available, the Parisian one. Today that "classic" pornographic novel, endowed with all the merits of an eighteenth-century style, can be bought in paperback anywhere in America. I will not take it upon myself to say whether this is because the book has been acknowledged as a "work of art" or because the line dividing works with artistic aims from those without such aims has become hopelessly blurred. The author, John Cleland, who wrote the book for money and who later tried to redeem that youthful indiscretion by composing pious tracts, would be more than a little surprised were he to see that lark of his ranked with Homer's rhapsodies. The book's aim is quite limited: it presents sexual exercises in the most tempting possible light and could probably serve as a stimulant for bored lovers and sluggish married couples. Moreover, the passing of time has lent Cleland's novel almost bucolic features. One reads it with nostalgia because of its flagrantly artificial realism and its affirmation of simple pleasures enjoyed without hatred for the world.

The works of the Marquis de Sade, including his *Philosophy in the Bedroom,* are also available in paperback, and what is of interest to me is my instinctive opposition. I allow for two possibilities here: either my mind, formed by Catholicism, Marxism, or simply by Europe's historical convulsions, is somewhat totalitarian and silently accepts the idea that the spiritual nourishment given the "masses" should be controlled; that is, it usurps the knowledge of what is healthy and unhealthy for them. Or, as a result of the distance I have on the morals prevailing around me, I dare to detect a problem where others do not because it would be inconvenient. *Philosophy in the Bedroom* is undoubtedly the most immodest work of literature ever written, and not because it depicts an aristocratic circle collectively sampling all forms of copulation, with a marked predilection for sodomy. The dialogue form lends the work a quality of parody, of *opera buffa,* and one reads it with a smile, though one that soon gives way to boredom, since the endless descriptions of erotic frenzy are monotonous.

But Sade is also proposing a new morality and thus is a forerunner of the Surrealists who published poetry in honor of the poisoner, Violette Nozières. Divine and human laws were invented to deprive the individual of his natural privileges. Liberating himself from lies and hypocrisy, the perfect libertine appoints his own pleasure as the sole standard of good and evil. Divine and human laws cannot, however, be overthrown effectively until they are attacked at their very bases, the point where they are automatically accepted by everyone. Even the most daring philosopher shudders before crossing a certain line. Only the readiness to commit murder for one's own pleasure proves that the Commandments, those completely artificial fetters, have been left behind. *Philosophy in the Bedroom* is a treatise on murder. The sixteen-year-old Eugénie is initiated by degrees; at first, sexually, but later on, when she is emboldened to begin breaking down the prohibitions imparted to her at home, she is eager for further lessons. She learns that one is free to kill. But it is commonly held that there is something worse than killing a human being, and Eugénie passes her examination in another fashion: she admits that she hates her bigoted mother and joyfully consents to the plan for punishing her. She looks on, clapping her hands, as her mother is lured to the château and raped, not only to humiliate her but also to infect her with syphilis.

The fate of the Marquis de Sade shows us that a public opinion bound to a definite moral code was ill disposed to such philosophical proposals and that it displayed great self-confidence in combating them. While the printing of such works as *Philosophy in the Bedroom* for mass consumption can be explained as a weakening of the standards of judgment, another factor probably weighs more heavily here: the unspoken assumption that the influence of the written word on institutions and morals is small or nonexistent.

Everything I have written so far about censorship seems completely old-fashioned to me, as old-fashioned as regimes in which the state pays a large number of functionaries solely to pencil out whole sentences from novels or, when the need arises, to improve a poet's verses. One must be able to see the printed page along with everything else that surrounds us in quantities that would have confounded our ancestors. Such multitudes of people, ideas, media, goods produced by technology and thrown out half-consumed! The Marquis de Sade was a total revolutionary, the most radical of the radical, and he set about his philosophical enterprise seriously. But his books, like books in general, now fill a different function than they did once. They are exhibits in an enormous, constantly expanding museum in which works of art from all civilizations and epochs—codexes, Bibles, Korans—are neighbors in a syncretic turmoil. The most extreme injunctions neutralize and demolish each other, immediately turning into "culture." The technical apparatus which produces the spoken, written, and pictorial language intercepts and co-opts every revolt for its own use, including the revolt against it. The programs of anarchists, predictions of the end of the world, cries for political assassination, exhortations to flee to the forests and mountains in order to devote oneself to contemplation, the advertisements of leagues whose members meet naked and "experience others' essence," drug propaganda, hymns in honor of totalitarian regimes—all have equal rights and satisfy the needs of the market. A dash of apocalypse or revolution livens up the market, and were it lacking, it would be necessary to invent it for commercial purposes.

Censorship as prohibition loses its *raison d'être* when the tangible, material world remains resistant to everything stated in terms of "as if"; that is, to language, concepts, symbols. The tangible, material world can manage without ideas, which are replaced by ubiquitous necessity. Man as an economic creature behaves in one way rather than in another, not because philosophical generalizations arise in his head, but because he must satisfy his needs and can do so only by submitting to laws independent of his will. Such at least appears to be the hidden premise allowing one to relate with more tolerance than hostility to culture, to the museum, to treat it as something that "satisfies intellectual curiosity" and also softens the severity of life. This is a somewhat dubious premise, since the means of mass communications—i.e., language—are the driving force of an economy that is constantly creating new needs with the aid of advertising. Moreover, it is not certain whether the ideas locked in the reservoir of "culture" will always be content to remain there.

The Marquis de Sade, rendered less shocking by his status as a literary classic and by his antiquated style, is also further neutralized by new rivals in extremity who keep appearing every day. The sex and violence in his writings are a bit too conventional, not photographic enough. It is not often that the public's apathy, a result of constant bombardment, is overcome and some measure of renown achieved. Bluntness, brevity, and brutality of expression, as well as simplified ideas, are prized because they can be conveyed by the most obvious and tangible "facts" without involving any complicated reasoning. These requirements are exactly the opposite of those found in systems where the market is scorned, where language becomes a labyrinth of mutable meanings, where the censorship frugally portions out "facts," though great effort goes into their interpretation. The language of naturalistic, almost clinical description seems particularly effective in the struggle for attention and money, whereas the interpretation of a given work is built into its very structure, concealed; that is, the phenomena described tend to pass for actual reality. This has to favor the loud and garish; i.e., sex and violence get center stage. The word, moreover, is in competition with still and moving pictures, which are winning the race for expressive power and in turn yield to the demands of the highest bidder.

Our eyes are spared nothing. Scenes which not long ago could be found only in the novels of Cleland or Sade are right here before me on the screen. The suffering people inflict upon each other, murder, mass slaughter, war, can be seen while we are sitting at home (on color television). Whether someone is committing murder or being murdered makes no difference: you watch. Nor does it matter if the author, director, or photographer wants to stimulate or to warn, since the means used are the same. The film *Bonnie and Clyde* may be taken as an example of this ambiguity. The story of a pair of criminals is presented as "real history," with naturalistic accuracy, which does not at all mean that it has no "tendency," to use an old expression. The viewer is given an unflattering picture of the small towns of the American Midwest in the 1930's. The horrifying spiritual emptiness, the meaninglessness of life reduced to chasing after a livelihood, leaves the more imaginative individual only one way out, crime, the heroic epos of trampled souls. Possibly all of America was like that then, although one suspects that a shift from today to yesterday has taken place here, because this is exactly how younger, educated Americans see life in a small town—stunted, debased, meaningless—and they will flee from it anywhere, even to Hollywood. The film *Bonnie and Clyde*, as opposed to the real Bonnie and Clyde, who, it seems, were considerably more prosaic bandits, is about poor people divested of their human heritage who shoot other people because that is the only way they can regain their dignity, their right to hope. The hero's sexual impotence is obviously symbolic, indicat-

ing his inner rejection of poverty and fundamental deprivation. Thus, this is a film of social criticism, different from
the films of social criticism made before World War II, like
The Grapes of Wrath: they stressed injustice and material
poverty, while here, in keeping with another intellectual
fashion, the emphasis is on alienation, spiritual poverty.
Not the least and perhaps even the most essential aspect
of the film are the hunks of bloody, agonized flesh, in color,
all that which the camera would not have dared to show a
few decades ago. Not to mention the film's educational influence: for the students at Berkeley, *Bonnie and Clyde*
was a spectacle arousing pity and terror, a film against
violence and indirectly against the war in Vietnam. But
certainly many others who saw it were stimulated in other
ways, delighting in the poetry of rebellion and the well-
aimed pistol shots. The point is that neither the former nor
the latter will ever be able to erase those hunks of bloody
flesh from their imagination.

Our imagination has a greater capacity than that of previous generations. Horror was then, as it is now, a part of
existence, but formerly things were arranged so that horror
was screened off from everyday life. Even in the most sinister countries—industrializing England, for example, which
inspired Karl Marx's wrath—there were zones of gentleness and tranquillity. In Russia, the Siberian penal colonies
remained an obscure menace, and even Dostoevsky in his
House of the Dead omitted a great deal. Accounts of the
poverty of peasants seemed like news from some exotic
country. The hunting of Negroes in Africa and the transportation of slaves undoubtedly troubled the minds of
Europe's inhabitants, yet not all that much, since it happened far away and their eyes were not exposed to the

suffering. People were killed in war, but no one filmed it live. Humanity was divided into those who spoke but knew or wanted to know little, and those who knew a great deal but were silent.

All the bedrooms, all the battlefields! Buddhists burning themselves alive in protest against the war died in an arena greater than any in ancient Rome. And in Vietnam, also for the first time, the enemy has been fired upon and men have fallen while being filmed. The Europeans, inclined to self-pity, whose memories have retained incredible scenes, may have felt themselves robbed, since the knowledge of certain dismal features of human nature had ceased to be the exclusive property of those directly participating in the events. Did we not see, while drinking beer, the chief of the Saigon police kill an officer of the Vietcong, a prisoner of war, by shooting him in the temple? Did we not see Oswald, shot by Ruby, clutch at his stomach? Did we not see children burned by napalm? And Robert Kennedy falling the second after Sirhan shot him?

Many years ago, right after the war, during my first stay in America, I had a conversation with a certain famous writer, no doubt a humanitarian, about the Negro ghettos. From him I heard that, in spite of everything, things were getting better and better. My surprise stayed with me for a long time after that conversation: why did he say that, he whose works, translated into many languages, were like ancient tragedies told in prose? Did even he have to arrange things so that the truth was deleted from his mind, like those many Europeans I knew who did not wish to learn of the prisons and concentration camps, since that would have weakened their faith in their party or leader? Things have not been much simplified for gentle liberals of that writer's type, for the hellish aura of the ghettos and the barracks for farm workers emanates from the television, settling like a toxic mist on the living-room furniture.

It would be naïve to forget the great poverty of current information and the various edits made by a censorship which works behind the scenes, but often in the open as well. That, however, is not a poverty of "facts"; the more shocking they are, the more marketable. And so the imagination must accommodate pain, debasement, violence, poverty, the absurdity of beliefs and morals the whole world over, nothing is placated, nothing tamed by thought, which, after all, does cure us of our anxiety a little if, asking "Why," we receive an answer beginning: "Because." The world beats on us like unreason incarnate, like the creation of some mad gigantic brain. Can one accept that entire burden and agree that what is simply is, and that's that? One can, but only by ruminating in a state of brutish contemplation like a cow. If we are capable of compassion and at the same time are powerless, then we live in a state of desperate exasperation. Here surely is one of the causes of that ferocity which I have elsewhere called neo-Manichaean.

The Agony of
the West

My principal concern is the unacknowledged, barely conscious premises of my own thinking, or anyone else's. Besides belief in evolution, those premises include a negative valuation of the direction one's country, society, and civilization is taking. It is somewhat strange to write this while living in the country that has achieved the greatest economic power in history, but—judging by the rage and contempt emanating from books, paintings, and films—never before have so many people taken up indictment as a pastime. Although I feel a certain kinship with them, it is that precisely which inclines me to mistrust myself somewhat, for their activities are a mirror in which I can easily see myself.

A conviction of the decadence, the rotting of the West, seems to be a permanent part of the equipment of enlightened and sensitive people for dealing with the horrors accompanying technological progress. That conviction is as old as modern art. Here a single reference, Baudelaire's

114

cité infernale, will suffice. However, as soon as we assume that a regression is in fact occurring, the question arises—a regression from what, where is that ideal state of equilibrium and vigor for which we are supposed to yearn?

This question has met with the most diverse answers. The first great patron of the dissatisfied was, of course, Rousseau, who opposed the views of Hobbes, which were shared by the sober disciples of Reason. According to Hobbes, man had emerged from primordial savagery, barbarism, the uncontrolled struggle of everyone against everyone else. Before Rousseau, it hadn't entered anyone's mind to take the legend of the Golden Age literally and to dream of a state of nature without arts or sciences. Admittedly, Rousseau did not recommend a return to the condition of the innocent savage; he chose that state only as a model for consciously cultivated Virtue—the Virtue in whose name so many heads were soon to roll from the guillotine.

Tolstoy, Rousseau's disciple, in many respects outdid his master in the finality of his judgments. Perhaps Berdyaev was right in calling Tolstoy the evil genius of Russia, for the sage of Yasnaya Polyana trained the Russian intelligentsia in the advancing of absolute demands and in what may be called impatience with institutions, hierarchies, gradual improvement, with history in general as a fabric of imperfect good and imperfect evil, interwoven, interdependent.

But Tolstoy and Rousseau are just two of many answers. The Romantics were much taken with the Middle Ages, and from then on, the idealized image of an organic, patriarchal civilization welded together by the religious fervor of everyone, from kings to commoners, has reappeared frequently. Other romantics, known as utopian socialists, discovered the panacea for evil in the collective ownership of primitives who had no concept of private property, and tried to revive it in their phalansteries. The young Marx came to the conclusion not only that man does not live as he should but that the conditions in which he finds himself have alienated him from his essence, his humanity; hence the further conclusion (not altogether a logical one—rather, an act of faith) that a set of conditions assuring the unity of essence and existence must exist somewhere. Marx located those conditions in the past, in primitive communism, and in the future, in industrial communism. However, technological progress in the nineteenth century cared little for the plans of visionaries and revolutionaries; there was something automatic about it, and the popularity of science fiction exemplified by the optimistic novels of Jules Verne spoke more to the popular imagination than did angry treatises.

Only when science fiction begins to be laced with anxious forebodings and to fashion anti-utopias from them can one speak of the surfacing of latent currents of despair. Toward the end of his long life, H. G. Wells, till then always faithful to his scientific-humanitarian visions, published a small, despairing book, *Mind at the End of Its Tether*, in which he confessed that he saw little chance for humanity, entangled in its own inventions, to survive. His *Mind at the End of Its Tether* is nothing other than Allen Ginsberg's "Moloch whose name is the Mind."

Perhaps Europe's decadentism was inaugurated in 1886, the year the magazine *Le Décadent* appeared in Paris. The authors grouped around this magazine declared that they wished not to create but to destroy, for the hyper-blasé civilization of the West was dying and could no longer be saved. But the flower of decadentism had only begun to bud. It was nourished by various forces, chief among them the crisis in religion. Roughly at that same time, the deification of art as the loftiest sacral activity began to filter outward from small groups of bohemians to wider circles; no longer by what it communicated, but by its very form, art was to be a religion and the artist its priest. Thereafter, more and more people would contribute to the general confusion, opposing the cult of their own cult to a world without gods and a civilization without promise, while arguing fiercely about which of the quickly changing artistic "isms" made the most suitable substitute for the liturgy. A new, enormous field was opened up for dilettantes and idlers, since anyone who had finished high school felt in his heart that he was an artist, or at least qualified to hold forth on art.

I have no doubt that my mind imbibed all the ingredients of that despair in European civilization. My childhood coincided with the First World War, which marked the end of an order splendid in the opinion of some, rotten in the opinion of others, but an order nonetheless. The Russian Revolution followed, initiating an era of comparisons: "there-here." The nineteenth century's discouragements, disenchantments, gloomy prophecies, previously pushed to the side by the established order, now grew more distinct and crystallized, attacking my maturing mind from all sides. The old romantic yearning for hieratic societies of priests and knights came back to life in Oswald Spengler (who had a predecessor in the Russian Nikolai Danilevsky), who saw civilizations as organisms experiencing childhood, maturity, and the senility of old age.

Obviously, the West had already entered the ebb phase of its life forces. Defeated Germany radiated harsh and scornful tidings of the impasse into which Western man had been thrust by overweening Reason; hope was sought in Oriental sages, Hinduism, Buddhism. England's young writers, T. E. Hulme, T. S. Eliot, programmatically reverted to the past, seeing only sterility and boredom in the present, a wasteland of "hollow men" deprived of religious faith and thus of purpose and meaning in existence.

This doesn't mean that I was reading Spengler or that I knew anything about England. Still, tendencies of that sort were not alien even to Poland, infiltrating there through the writings of pre-revolutionary Russians; and since I knew some French, I learned about the invasion of pessimism from books written by devotees of Cartesian clarity, mainly conservatives, who, like Henri Massis (*Défense de l'Occident*), saw the Germans as the breeding ground of the epidemic. At the same time, the world was being inundated by revolutionary propaganda on "the decay of capitalism" and its inevitable death agony. Hitler's counterrevolution seemed the complete corroboration of those slogans. As for the Second World War, it fulfilled to excess the predictions of the prophets of decline, no matter what their assumptions. Never before in such a short span of time had so many millions of human beings been put to death, never before had the coldly planned destruction of entire nations had such perfected technical means at its command.

How Western Europe has functioned from the day the war ended until today, as I write, is a perfect mystery to me, in spite of the fact that I lived there, in France, for ten years, from 1950 to 1960. The European spirit hated itself, turned against itself, and derided the institutions it had elaborated, perhaps thus masking a painful sense of its own disgrace. It was an orgy, a pandemonium of all the disgust, bitterness, and hangovers I had known from my early youth, and which only now seem to have become fully acknowledged, revindicated, and justified with the help of fashionable discourses on *la nausée*, the absurd, alienation. That spirit rejected any "here and now," praising to the skies a "there and a sometime"; it was axiomatic that the West was moribund. "There" most frequently meant Russia, occasionally some other country where the Communists were in power; "sometime" meant mankind's voyage to the Islands of Happiness after the private means of production had been abolished and essence and existence had fused into one.

But while Europe's spirit was spending its energy on escape, its body was eating, drinking, and buying automobiles and refrigerators (by the grace of America, which for a long time had to keep the European economy in an "iron lung" and provide it artificial nourishment). That duality should induce some reflection, for it shakes somewhat Europe's established opinion about the interaction of the spirit and body of a given human community. If only it had been restricted to small groups of the chosen who were engaged in what is best defined by the French word *ricaner*, "to laugh venomously." But the mood of impotence, linked with sullen buffoonery, reached the masses from poetry and philosophy via the novel, the theater, film, and the press. It is not difficult to establish how themes and forms migrated from the elite genres, the abstruse treatises and hermetic poetry that made little sense to the general public, to the mass media. What the theater of the absurd brought to the stage had been known to readers of poetry for quite some time. The novel diluted and simplified experiments at first only appreciated by the initiated. Film entered into competition with the novel, the language of images lending an often fantastic power to the feeling of disgust; Fellini and Antonioni, for example, borrowed their themes from philosophers, primarily their angry attacks on (evil) existence cut off from the (good) human essence. Someone from another planet wishing to evaluate Western Europe by what it thought of itself would be forced to say that a revolution was coming and that renewed mutual slaughter would at least bring those Western Europeans a certain relief. However, it turned out just the other way around, and what seemed a poison became an agent of affluent stabilization.

America is separated from Europe only by the Atlantic, which is not very much. America's technical know-how in recent decades has been, among other things, engaged in assimilating European ideas. For, after all, those ideas are served by the extraordinary growth of higher education and the production of paperback books so furious that, as a New York publisher once told me, they're shoveled into storerooms like coal. This means that sixteen-year-olds become acquainted with Beckett and Ionesco in their school theater and soon encounter Nietzsche and Marx, Spengler, Sartre, Camus, as well as anti-utopias of every sort, in inexpensive editions. In other words, whatever the innumerable advocates of American purity for whom Europe has always been only a source of evil may think, the myth of decline and decay has to be contagious. I say myth because there is obviously a certain unity of aura and tone stronger than truth or untruth at work here. Besides, it would be difficult to separate the European and American contributions. American by birth, T. S. Eliot, now required reading, was an exponent of the dark, plaintive tone on both sides of a diminished ocean, and he was hardly an exception.

A cheerful young giant, a child in the cradle strangling centaurs, with an ever more splendid future before it—that portrait of America is ultimately mythical too. And we will probably commit no great error in assuming that a country like that which Walt Whitman created in *Leaves of Grass* never existed and that it derived from his imagination, like the urban wilderness with an inaccessible center—Balzac's Paris. Nevertheless, Whitman's intoxication with forward movement and space corresponded to the mood of the pioneers and settlers whose labors were rewarded in material success. But almost from its beginning, almost at its foundations, America dreamed of Arcadia, of a harmonious life in concord with nature, of the self-sufficient individual, happy and honest only when he takes just as much as he needs from nature with his ax and rifle, shunning society and the always-corrupt state. Whitman, too, glorified this Adam. And Thoreau, who believed the civilized New Englanders bore their lot as men with "quiet desperation," established something of an archetype for American intellectuals by preaching civil disobedience and fleeing to his log cabin on a forest lake. And I, who was raised on tart and bitter European dishes, am now surrounded by new Thoreaus who differ from their spiritual forebear in considering the "quiet desperation" of their millions of fellow citizens to be the result of an increasingly cybernetic civilization, and who, while spitefully awaiting that direction to be proven wrong, quote Nietzsche or Marx, or something lifted from biology on the birth and withering of organisms.

The Formless
and the New

If I did not live here, where fashions, both intellectual and otherwise, originate and then spread across the whole of America, I would probably be asking myself somewhat different questions. I would be less certain that something still unnamed and absolutely new is now emerging, and I would say, along with everyone, that every new generation puts its antics behind it after sowing its wild oats, and the social order, having been momentarily disturbed, reasserts its rights. Here, however, one can see all too clearly how a small group of like-minded people has changed into a large group and then into a throng. The initial models were provided by the writers and artists who turned away from a vulgar dollars-and-cents civilization and retreated to the wild Pacific coast, to the area known as Big Sur near the small town of Carmel. That was in the forties. Then, in the fifties, the Beatniks appeared, both a San Francisco school of poets and a way of life. The scornful rebellion of the Beatniks was not without its influence, and their works combined with other factors to prepare the next mutation. In the mid-sixties, Haight and Ashbury streets in San Francisco were called "Hippieland"; despairing parents from

all over America began to travel there in search of their run-
away teenage sons and daughters.

But a great deal had happened even before then. The
teachings of various gurus preaching Zen Buddhism found
a great response among the renegades from the dying, for-
mal religions, who, as a rule, were only dimly aware of the
bases of Christianity and Judaism; besides, this Oriental
wisdom was, as a rule, obtained second- or third-hand from
European literature, which caused a resurgence of fame for
Hermann Hesse, author of *Steppenwolf* and other such novels (at the time they were written, they aroused the indig-
nation of the French, who saw the Germans as carriers of
the Oriental plague); were it not for the far-flung popularity of Hesse's books, there would be no Café Steppenwolf in Berkeley. Along with inducements to travel into the
depths of one's soul, there also developed an enormous
underground market for "consciousness-expanding" sub-
stances; the church and synagogue were equated with the
mental inertia of the older generation, and the alcohol culture was seen as the symbol of its customs; therefore, the
renunciation of alcohol and its replacement by the marijuana culture had the distinct features of cementing a
group, especially since absurd legislation caused the herb
to acquire its prophets and martyrs. True, soon enough it
would become a public secret that ever-larger numbers of
respectable citizens preferred marijuana to alcohol. There
is nothing surprising about Aldous Huxley's book in defense of peyote and mescaline having been written in California. The experiments conducted there would soon be a
nearly normal part of the initiation rites of the young generation, especially with the discovery of lysergic acid,

which could be produced in even the most meager laboratory. A trip under the influence of lysergic acid requires the
assistance of a guide who knows the successive stages that
each "tripper" passes through; it was a short way from
there to rituals—ecstatic gatherings, with their mélange of
Oriental music, Hasidic handclapping, and Indian dances:
they dreamed of brotherhood with the Indians, whose religion commended the use of those narcotics providing a
sense of the One and All-Embracing, the Indians perse-
cuted by generations of white Americans of the Christian-
alcohol culture. Fashions were adopted from the Indians—
long hair for men, tied with headbands; necklaces of metal
or beads; designs painted on faces. But it should also not be
forgotten that all this occurred simultaneously with a very
swift increase in poets, sculptors, painters, potters, etc.; in
any case, people proclaiming that they wanted to devote
themselves to contemplation and creativity, not to making
money. For my parents' generation, America was the land
of the Golden Calf, while today it is clearly becoming the
most poetic and artistic country in the world.

"Subcultures" might interest a sociologist or delight lovers of the peculiar, but I do not number myself in either
category. Different varieties of subcultures appear and disappear, as shown by the so-called Existentialists who con-
gregated in Parisian *caves* right after the Second World
War. In its most striking forms, the movement I am discussing is just such a transitory subculture, or, rather, it is one
that melts into the general flow of fashion. It is important
only in that it is one of the symptoms of America's split into
two mutually hostile parts.

What does it mean if in one country or another a student
—till then obedient, neat, crew-cut, pursuing a definite

goal; i.e., a well-paying profession—becomes a synonym for subversion? If, long-haired and bearded, he rejects all the religious, social, and political values that his parents hold, searches for the meaning of life, listens to incomprehensible music, and devotes himself to inconceivable experiments with drugs? And what if the boundary between political subversive, vagabond, student, poet, singer of original ballads, and even Indian is erased as it was for the hippies whom I picked up hitchhiking on Euclid Avenue recently? And what if not only in San Francisco but in cities significantly less amenable to such things entire neighborhoods spring up populated by people not fussy about their housing, who live on milk and fruit, walk around in tattered sweaters, but, on the other hand, have time to read, write, paint, and do not take part in the "rat race"?

Could I be witnessing a rebirth of *fin de siècle* bohemia? Everything, the dress, the disgust for the average man, the philosophical reveries, would indicate that I am. Yes, but there were very few European bohemians, and they went almost unnoticed by the philistines they held in contempt. Here, where instead of a few dozen *poètes maudits*, hundreds of thousands adopt that style of thought and life, not only quantity but quality is changed. I have heard the opinion that this is just another one of history's jokes, that the anti-machine ferment arising in America, despite the predictions about a general leveling, may well be, in fact, the wholly legitimate child of the machine. Its appearance corresponds exactly in time with the onset of automation, which will deprive ever larger numbers of people of work. However, because the goods produced in automated factories will have to be sold, the state will guarantee everyone a decent pension; i.e., earning money will become separated from working. There will thus ensue a division of people into those few responsible for the proper functioning of the machines and a majority enjoying the right of no responsibility. But for the average American citizen, at his current level, freedom from all work would threaten madness; even assuming that Adam's burden could be lifted and he could return to Paradise, all the hours he had spent running around to make a living could not be filled by sex, fishing, and stamp collecting. This new movement would thus seem to be a sign of man's instinctive ability to adapt to constantly changing circumstances; the philosophical and poetic bohemians always knew how to find a multitude of interesting ways to spend their time, managing without the yoke which, in their opinion, rightly burdens the stupid squares.

According to the opinion just expressed, which may or may not be correct, we are dealing here with the vanguard of the future making its appearance disguised as decadence. There is much to be said for that interpretation. Moloch, considered hideous and inhuman by the longhairs, does not and will never, in their opinion, submit to human control; rather, it is Moloch who swallows up those who would like to control him. All that remains is to withdraw, so that his breath poisons us as little as possible, and to divest oneself of responsibility. At the same time, however, the power of Moloch's existence is never questioned: the outward sign of that respect is the use of money, which the short-haired servants of Moloch earn and the longhairs spend. Whatever the moral contradictions here, there is no doubt that this entire movement could not have arisen in a poor country. Blacks, generally poor of necessity, do not look too fondly on the ideologues of insouciance, despite viewing them as allies in revolt against everything which gives the whites pleasure.

A safety valve, a growing fringe? It might just as easily be something else entirely. One cannot draw a line between the attitudes of resignation and withdrawal and those of active revolt, just as at one time in Europe it was difficult in the artists's cafés to decide who was all talk and who the professional revolutionary. The many thousands of meetings, sit-ins, anti-war marches, attract both those restoring bohemia on a mass scale and those who are activists and organizers by temperament. A few years ago in Berkeley, watching fourteen thousand students sitting on the stone benches of the Greek Theater reacting with one great hostile shout at the speech by the university's president, Clark Kerr (a liberal), I realized that, to understand any of this, one would have to measure it by another country, another century. The strength of the collective emotion was not in proportion to the causes of their dissatisfaction, trivial if viewed rationally, and the very name of the student confederation, the Free Speech Movement, would not have meant anything to European students, who are for the most part disregarded and do not enjoy many rights. That was a vicarious discharge: the university authorities were treated as the representatives of authority in general. The students in the Greek Theater were united by the tacit and, for them, obvious premise that any authority issuing from an evil system and protecting that system was itself pure evil. Isn't this the nineteenth-century Russian intelligentsia? In Russia, views that are publicly expressed in America would have meant prison, Siberia; the Russian revolutionary organizers did not have walkie-talkies at their disposal either, a very useful tool at mass demonstrations of various sorts. Nevertheless, if we take the principal characteristic of the Russian intellectual to be the conviction that in the name of moral principles one must condemn "them"—i.e., the supports of the system—and that any reforms proposed by them have to be a lie since pure evil is not cured with half measures, the similarity becomes explicit. There are also counterparts to the peasant problem, which are quite compelling, at least emotionally—the blacks, the Indians relegated to barren reservations, the Mexican farm workers in California. This does not mean that history is repeating itself and that the formation of a monastic order of the spiritually afflicted similar to Russia's has to produce similar consequences. The circumstances are different, as is the "acceleration of history." Universal prosperity has little attraction as an ideal here because it has been "their" ideal. Moreover, this dissent from the state is transpiring in a country where the state was always viewed with suspicion and where anarchy was conspicuous for its remarkable efficiency in organizing itself "from the bottom up."

The larger fish consume the smaller: the concentration of capital is borne out by the example of the press. The weaker newspapers go under, taken over by large chains. Thus, the success of the papers of the "underground press," differing from their European namesakes in that they are sold on street corners, was a surprise, the result of the long-haired editors, contributors, and buyers. One of those numerous publications, *The Berkeley Barb*, is for me the strangest reading in the world, though I have happened upon all sorts of bizarre oddities in print. Besides, it illustrates what I said a moment ago about the lack of distinct demarcations between the bohemians who withdrew and the revolutionary intelligentsia. The language used by the *Barb* would certainly present problems for anyone knowing only proper English, it is the spoken language, dialect in full bloom. In the *Barb* I have read a great many articles about the state of mystical unity with the godhead, attained with the help of "consciousness-expanding" drugs, as well as a long treatise proving that Jesus used hashish; it also prints many articles about the new principles of collective life discovered and tried out by the flower children, information about their gatherings, liturgies, centers for mutual aid, and so on. While the *Barb* is intended for those who preserve their own islands of gentleness, goodness, and brotherhood amid the inhuman machines, there are also fifteen minutes of hate in every issue. The subject of that hatred is all those who are in power, beginning with the brutal local police and ending at the White House, whose occupant has been transformed by virulent drawings and unflattering epithets, to say the least, into the very sign and symbol of crime. The young blacks of the Black Panther organization have contributed very effectively to the fifteen minutes of hate by proclaiming that every "whitey" is, whether he wishes to be or not, a criminal. As for theoretical discourses on revolutionary action, the Establishment politicians expected nothing of the sort. Quite a few years ago I was honored by the confidence of the European "situationists," who sent me the first issue of their magazine *Internationale Situationiste*. This was before the Dutch "Provos," offshoots of that same Internationale, had started making trouble, and before the "situationists" had given all France hell. The radical rejection of technical-industrial civilization, both the American and the Russian versions, the slogan of total revolution which would liberate man from alienation, Marx but not Lenin—all that, too, went into the *Barb*'s varied and often self-contradicting proposals, plus sarcasm directed at conservative, that is, Communist ideas, and support for a cult of romantic figures—Fidel Castro, Che Guevara, Ho Chi Minh.

All that chaos would have been relatively familiar to someone raised in Europe like myself, were it not for one other ingredient, one alien to the European revolutionary tradition—sex. The *Barb*'s contributors seem to profess the principle that "there is no universal revolution without universal copulation," as the Marquis de Sade puts it in Weiss's play *Marat/Sade*. That is why the *Barb* allots considerable space to propaganda for a society called the Sexual Freedom League, to numerous descriptions of its get-togethers (access to which is easy, provided all clothes and fig leaves are left behind in the front hall), debates on the philosophical meaning of nudity, a new code of proper behavior. I especially remember one article which lodged a complaint about male egoism. The author, a woman, related how at the ebb of one of those gatherings, near morning, the woman of the house came downstairs and addressed the dozen or so young people, already sexually sated and dozing on the sofas, requesting one of them to bestow his favors on one last girl, who was waiting upstairs in the bedroom. No one budged: chivalry and gallantry were truly dead! The *Barb* also has a section of advertisements which are almost exclusively sexual. Some of them are striking in their business-like brevity ("Male wants a female"), but a significant percentage boast of the endowments of young men ready to serve, for a modest fee, one may assume. Of all places—in the "underground press," which would seem ill-disposed to the efficient organization of capitalist enterprises—but the young businessmen come right to the point as if they were opening up a new gas station. However, the "underground press" has to survive too, and it has hit upon a redeeming formula—revolution mixed with sex. Some mass-market publications, lavishly printed on expensive paper, have also borrowed this discovery, ingeniously mixing doses of pornography, avant-garde literature, and left political rage. Now, when the two Americas are beginning to assume more distinct contours in our minds, once again everything becomes embroiled and unclear, since we cannot be sure that the editors of all those *Barbs* will not end their careers as smiling priests of Moloch.

The Evangelical
Emissary

Slowly, indirectly, I am approaching the proper theme of
my book. But before I proceed to gather and tie up the
various strands, let Holy Hubert appear on these pages. For
several years this small, freckled man has stood every day
at his post by the entrance to the university campus in
Berkeley. He is an evangelist, a preacher of the teachings of
Jesus. I have practically never seen him speak calmly. He is
usually thrashing about in something like a trance, red-
faced, with swollen veins and drops of sweat on his dan-
druff-covered forehead; his noisy exhortations and thunder-
ings against sin do not carry very far because hoarseness
makes his voice break in a choked falsetto. He is such a
part of the colorful carnival atmosphere that practically no
one stops for him, never more than four or five listeners,
who regard him with mellow smiles and sometimes amuse
themselves by asking him questions if his enthusiasm slack-
ens and he has to be reexcited. He is a popular figure, a
part of the local folklore like the boys in their saffron robes
chanting "Rama Krishna, Krishna Rama" over and over,
and the students treat him with the benevolence one shows
the harmlessly insane.

Despite certain psychopathic traits, Holy Hubert is not

mentally ill, even though the complete uselessness of his dogged ministerings (for it is doubtful whether he has convinced even a single student) could prompt such suspicions. His mistake was that, instead of addressing the citizens in small towns in Arkansas or Kentucky, who would have listened to him with respect, he decided to become a missionary among people whose way of thinking is not accessible to him, so that even the religious students remain indifferent to his cries. Perhaps he wishes to imitate St. Paul preaching in pagan Athens, but he is completely unaware of any of the historical changes occurring now. He is an unwilling example of the aging of certain mental formations which continue to exist along with other fresher ones and which, in Arkansas, for example, are still taken completely seriously, while elsewhere, in Berkeley, they seem like parodies. If the supporters of Ho Chi Minh or members of the Black Panthers begin speaking on the steps of Sproul Hall near the spot on the sidewalk Holy Hubert works, a fervent, excited crowd forms at once, and that alone ought to cause Hubert to reflect, though obviously he could explain all that to himself in his own way.

The absurdity of behavior like Hubert's, playfully nicknamed "Holy" by the students, may deserve sympathy, although he is not devoid of humor and he clearly needs to blow off steam by yelling for his own health. My theme, which I am approaching indirectly, is the erosion of the system of ideas and customs which form the American way of life. Hubert, in some sense, is a delegate from the traditional morality sent out among the apostates and sinners. The battle of the police against marijuana in the vicinity of the campus is another example of such holding actions.

Describing his states after taking hashish in his treatise

Les Paradis Artificiels, Baudelaire contributed to a new variety of tale about witches and ghosts. The heroes of those tales were bohemian artists appalling the philistines with their readiness to make pacts with the devil. The paintings and literary works of these bohemians were finally recognized as precursors and included in "culture," but their customs were thought of as characteristic of a certain epoch forever past. In the Europe of my youth, impressed by the seriousness of political upheavals, no one would have believed that bohemia, by its very way of life, was an augury of mass phenomena with social and political significance and that a time would come when Baudelaires, though not necessarily talented ones, would number in the hundreds of thousands or millions. Those who read Stanislaw Ignacy Witkiewicz's novels about the future thought there was something to his prophecies, but not when he predicted the great role narcotics would play (this was considered a private eccentricity on his part).

Taking a logical approach, there is no reason not to sentence people to death for smoking tobacco or to long prison sentences for drinking alcohol; those are dangerous drugs. But, although in certain countries tobacco had its martyrs who were hanged, the strict edicts against it have passed into oblivion, and after the failure of Prohibition in America, drinking has become a ritual that proves one a normal, decent, loyal citizen. Taking into account the fact that *Cannabis sativa* is, in comparison with tobacco and alcohol, a rather innocent substance, much ado about nothing, the stubbornness with which the police pursued marijuana throughout the sixties had the mark of an obsession like Hubert's zealous rantings. The searching of pockets, the handcuffs, the prison sentences can only be explained by a sense of threat from "others," and not without basis. It is doubtful whether the use of marijuana would have become so widespread had it not also served as a sort of tribal insignia for all those who questioned the established order.

I do not mean to slight the political potential of marijuana, if only because, like jazz, it came from the underground culture, the colored peoples. Black activists are trying to wipe out heroin, the plague of the ghetto, but everyone smokes marijuana. Moreover, the police ban on marijuana is causing the whites to draw nearer the blacks because of the similarity of their situations: to be a criminal means to look at society from the bottom, from underground, the way it is seen by blacks, who know the color of their skin makes them suspicious to the police.

Hubert's missionary zeal: unfortunately, while observing him, I cannot understand what makes him tick, and for me he is a sort of living puppet, not a pleasant way to think about another human being.

But at least, thanks to him, I can puzzle out how the two systems of ideas and customs, the old and the new, relate to each other. If it were up to me, I would prefer not to be forced to choose between them.

Henry Miller

I read Henry Miller's books some time ago, right after the war, and my reactions were dictated by my habits. I do not know whether those habits, which I still have not rid myself of, are praiseworthy or simply the biases common to my place of origin. Perhaps they are only biases, but I do not intend to conceal them, and so I should say, first, that I feel a perhaps inordinate respect for literature as a code. I do not think a writer's hand is entirely in the control of his will or even of his blind passions, another hand holds his and guides it across the paper, so that, whether he is conscious of it or not, his work, by the very way in which the words and sentences are connected, documents a place and a moment, while also serving some unfathomable purpose. That documenting is not without its ambiguity, and changes meaning, depending on other changes in that kaleidoscopic system of which every notation of each individual human voice becomes part. Second, the romantic legacy probably lies behind a certain conviction of mine; namely, that the human species, which lives in its own specific dimension, a cumulative one because of memory and time, has at every moment a certain optimum knowledge of itself, and that no eminence in philosophy or art is possible without aspiring to at least that optimum. I do not expect writers to prove that they are conversant with the currents, schools, and so on, or any philosophizing—the less cultural snobbery they have, the better. However, it does seem certain to me that a trained mind is qualitatively different from an untrained one, a point that needs no scholarly debates for its proof. Similarly, the traditional methods of training the mind are the best, though, in their caricatured form—the French *lycée*, for example—they were laughable.

Henry Miller was so extreme in opposing his own person to everything outside of it that he rejected literature as a collection of inherited patterns, in order to stand unique, to say a Mass to himself, to present the image of himself as a perfect male (Whitman, Hart Crane, Ezra Pound, Hemingway, all wrote "songs of themselves"). To me, that Miller seemed like a medium in a trance. A medium shouting, shaken by a powerful current, whose violent gestures, vulgarities, and floods of invective were clearly directed against some enemy, though his yammerings made it impossible to decide who or what that enemy was. The twentieth century? America? New York? Maxim Gorky visited New York before World War I and described it most unfavorably in his sketch "The City of the Yellow Devil." The Yellow Devil, gold. That was not an exaggerated satirical portrait, especially since Gorky identified with the wretchedly poor, the masses of immigrants; for them, life was desperately hard in that city, a far cry from the naïve fantasies of America they had cherished in their native villages. However, Gorky's portrait was too one-dimensional and is today only a relic of a certain critique of capitalism which somehow always managed to miss the bull's-eye. The Yellow Devil proved capable of miracles which Gorky could not foresee, and it was also for that reason that the rather large number of Gorky's fellow socialists on this continent did not achieve their goal. The enemy tormenting Miller in his hypnotic trance has no face or body, it cannot be caught, struck, wounded, it eludes names and diagnoses. Perhaps it is the technological civilization of the twentieth century, the supposed blind alley where we have been driven by our unhealthily active minds, or human society in general, or America—first it seems one, then the other, and the images flow into each other. In any case, it is Armageddon, and the trumpets of the Last Judgment can be heard above it. The individual should defend himself as best he can—by spitting and mocking as Miller did, even entitling a book on his travels through America *The Air-Conditioned Nightmare.*

Miller was one of the first prophets of withdrawal into the purely personal dimension, what we could call the sexual-mystical dimension, and as well one of the first in daily practice to withdraw from the round of "getting and spending" to a primitively furnished cabin in Big Sur. Perhaps I was not foolish to read him twenty years ago as a medium for nameless forces. There were still no Beatniks then, Allen Ginsberg had not published yet (his hysterical howl comes primarily from Miller), there were no hippies. Whatever Miller's influence has been (not very wide-ranging), it was not, after all, he himself who produced that host of kinsmen. They were called into being by the same forces which tore the indecent words from his lips.

Despite my awe of Miller, for who does not dream of being freed of all inner controls to sit at the typewriter and bang out whatever the saliva brings to the tongue, I never trusted him. There is something known as the humanistic tradition, and I am convinced that the optimum I referred to earlier cannot be achieved outside that tradition. Miller, a self-taught man, was, however, nourished not only by the sterile soil of his native Manhattan. He says himself that he grew up on the writings of Friedrich Nietzsche. And later he made considerable use of his Paris years; his writing technique was not, after all, born of itself—to a significant degree, it was taken from the French poet and prose writer Blaise Cendrars. But Nietzsche was a scholar with excellent training in the historical sciences, philology, a humanist in revolt against the stultifying ideas of the academies. Similarly, the verve and nonchalance of Cendrars (whose adventurousness in life may also have impressed Miller) had the experience of French grammarians and rhetoricians as their background; he stuck out his tongue at them, but despite that, he was connected to them by a multitude of links, even through his own resistance to them. Something disturbing occurs when Americans throw themselves on European authors, especially Nietzsche. The play of their contradictions disappears, a certain trait of humor hidden beneath their fury, which only the historical imagination provides, whereas what the Americans extract are the elements which allow them reconciliation with the ideal of the "natural man"; actually, the man of the natural sciences. Nietzsche, an unhappy Lucifer, proud and pure, found plebeian incarnation in Miller. As someone has remarked, fornication is the poetry of the masses. Miller brings no glad tidings, no *gaia scienza* to a humanity which he condemns to incipient chaos, meaninglessness, and, finally, extermination. Everything he did to make the situation of man in one time and place pass for man's general situation was too transparent, at least for someone who, like me, was once a catastrophist and was later to see with his own eyes the most doleful prophecies fulfilled, which, however, did not signify the end of the world but, unexpectedly, even revealed humanity's talent for rebirth.

The mind, so weighed down with scholarly formulations that it is intimidated, cowed, and does not trust itself, is certainly a plague, and Miller's volcanic roar, indifferent to all authority, is fascinating, exciting, and, like a Martian who has come across Earth's arts and sciences, he is sometimes dazzling in the freshness of his judgments. But his great writing talent masks the immature confusion in his mind. I only talked with Miller once, in Paris, probably in 1952. I did not like how avidly he predicted the end of the world. Besides, I was not lucky in my relations with him. In 1948 I promised to visit him in Big Sur, some obstacles arose, and I did not visit him. Later, in Paris, I promised to find him a rare book which contained a prophecy of catastrophe for the human race, *La Clef de l'Apocalypse* by O. V. de L. Milosz, which he had been hunting in the bookshops of the Latin Quarter. I did not find the book, I forgot my promise, I had too many troubles of my own at the time. Miller caustically reproached me for all this in his memoirs, where, with his usual lack of precision, he referred to me as the author of a large successful novel. The causes of this vindictiveness are rather plain. Miller demanded absolute admiration and did not like people in whom he sensed any reluctance, and he, perhaps rightly, saw my broken promises as a refusal to honor him.

I, Motor, Earth

Thus far, on all these pages, I may only have been approaching my subject, and as these are the last few chapters, I perhaps ought to include a short treatise on the automobile. Not the automobile as a motor, gearbox, speed, etc., or as a vehicle for moving about the city and for trips to the suburbs, but rather the automobile as a special instrument establishing a relationship between myself and the continent, between myself and the world. This is not explainable in terms of any similarities with European habits. It was only once, driving from Florence to Rome through the Campagna Romana wastes, that I felt in Europe something like an allusion to that unified trinity— I, motor, Earth. But even then I was headed somewhere, there was a destination; it is something else again when we are moving straight ahead into an endless void, populated here and there, and from time to time rising up into cities. If the goal is not sufficiently distinguished from what surrounds it, the pursuit of that goal is valid only as a decision arrived at, map in hand, but since no changes can be expected, the trip becomes no more than persistent motion, which at the same time makes it unclear whether we are moving or are immobile witnesses of a moving space dotted with identical gas stations, roadside restaurants, and motels. The cities: the band of freeway takes us over their symmetrical rectangles, or else they are simply obstacles, for they force us to slow down and stop at their traffic lights. The trip takes place inside the car, the only ultimate contact is with the car, and the trip is measured by the speedometer's needle and the numbers crawling past on the odometer; everything outside flashes by, appears and disappears, silvery, unreal, a screen. Perhaps the passengers on long-distance express trains and planes are also severed from reality in the same manner, but their passivity was accepted in advance and written into the contract, the ticket. The owner of an automobile is actively passive, with a constant desire for activity, for an activity other than holding the wheel, but he is continually being cast into passivity again. In the deserts of southern California and Arizona, the very thought of stopping for anything but gas or food seems absurd—why bother when you can see everything you need to out the window? There is nothing out there besides stunted, prickly vegetation. Though the coniferous forest in the Sierras is attractive, with its greenery and shade, it too, after a few steps, kills any desire for a walk amid its scree-covered tracts, rocks, inaccessible thickets. But our active passivity is also felt in relation to people. We pass them, busy with their daily work, immersed in their houses and little towns. We converse with them when we stop—in stores, restaurants, motels—but differently from the way people did when they traveled by camel, horse, or stagecoach. They do not bring us into their tents, they don't set out feasts in honor of their guests, who are precious because they are rare. The banal ritual of greetings and goodbyes, so smooth that we pass each other like pebbles rounded by a stream, puts a distance between us and them, and so their eyes, mouths, movements are all the more disturbing to us. They are enigmatically self-enclosed, and haunt our minds as if we were from another planet, staring at humans.

I-they. A fundamental opposition, the very heart of our human fate, sometimes obscured, often acute. I, a European; they, the Americans? But I am here for the very same reason they are, because things were bad in Europe, and I have no intention of forgetting that. Not enough attention is paid to the simple truth that average people have little time to acquire views and customs unrelated to their most immediate environment. Their horizons are defined by the curvature of the earth's surface as they see it from the doorways of their houses, and they take that with them if they go anywhere. That is not how I travel. In childhood, I was raised in a completely different civilization and then learned others—not from books, not only from books, but with my five senses. Even with that background I, a tourist in his car, do not make comparisons such as "In Europe, we . . . in America, you." For me, "I and they" simply means I and the people who live at the same time as I do. And so, actually, my treatise on the automobile ought to be entitled: "What is to be done with man?"

How many times have I said, in those little towns which are like nomad camps, so impermanent, so makeshift are their walls of painted plywood and neon: "It would be terrible to live here." Yet, if finding myself in the little town of Desert Center in the southernmost part of California, I viewed it with a certain appreciation, that was only because it had been so aptly named, though actually no one knows whether a desert can have a middle or a center. But the name was better than Eureka, Alcybiades, Syracuse, and almost as good as Malheur National Forest. It was in Desert Center as the waitress—her clothing, hair, and makeup all impeccable—was preparing the hamburgers that my annoyance at my undeserved superiority found its expression and form. For I considered her and everyone there mental cripples, and rightly so, unfortunately, as the simplest calculation will demonstrate. The hours spent each day at work not only do not allow them to break through their habits of mind, they consolidate them. Everything depends on submitting to a certain mass norm, they can only take what is given them, from lipsticks and deodorants to the magazines with their brightly colored covers, and television, which becomes richer in brutality and more moronic, the farther one goes from the big cities. Freedom of choice diminishes in proportion to the number of miles on the odometer. Statistics concerning the book business represent a national average, misleading since in all the towns like Desert Center there isn't a bookstore to be seen. The local newspapers serve up "facts"; but someone without instruction acquired elsewhere will not be able to make any intelligent connections among those facts. And yet this country consists primarily of such towns, their citizens vote for politicians who are clever but more often than not none too bright.

The provincial yokels and morons are hated by those with beards and long hair, and the feeling is mutual. The prescribed, normal banality of contact becomes grating if the traveler has a beard, the badge of moral and political otherness, whereas it turns almost cordial if the stranger is both clean-shaven and wearing a cowboy hat. I had not thought that I would have to repeat experiences already familiar to me and to many generations of Europeans. In Europe, and in Eastern Europe especially, as far back as the era of romanticism, people had been divided into the noble, pure spirits who dreamed of transforming man into an angelic being, and the vulgar herd, often simply referred to as swine. From then on, the cries of despairing poets and revolutionaries have rung out in protest against a life without a deeper justification. To be a member of the intellectual class clearly cut one off from the "masses," which were considered either incurably apathetic or else in need of being roused to action. Gradually, the bourgeoisie, then the peasants, ceased to be seen as a source of hope; now the proletariat got the attention because its fate seemed to make it the very incarnation of the idea of universal dialectical reason. The poetry of the young American poets is, for the most part, angry, and descriptions of trips by car through a hostile country occupy no small place in that poetry—hostile because here consciousness judges unconsciousness. This is reminiscent of the complaints of Russian poets horrified by a Russia of illiterate and superstitious peasants. However, there are no barefoot illiterates now, no peasantry, the categories of bourgeoisie and proletariat have blurred, with the exception of the proletariat branded by the color of its skin.

I understand what pains American youth, so full of hatred, so promethean and romantic. A French friend, a Parisian intellectual, having driven across the continent coast to coast, summed up her observations as follows: *"Mon Dieu, quel malheur."* She did not have to explain to me what she meant by that, for both she and I assume that man is pure potential; and it is bad if his potential is impeded to the degree that he has even been deprived of the language that could express his aspirations, for it has been replaced by the language of the mass media, which makes everything shallow and false. But the painful sense of some sort of lack does not disappear, and man suffers without realizing why. Occasionally, he catches a glimmer of an unattainable, genuine existence beyond his sham, inauthentic existence. Those repressed, stunted aspirations erupt from time to time, becoming blind aggression, as witnessed by the film *Bonnie and Clyde*. The *"malheur"* my French friend spoke of is perhaps nothing but the inability to complain. There is no grumbling, no pity for themselves. What is simply is. And, on the surface at least, everything is fine.

And thus "I and they" is nothing but an "intellectual" (of whatever sort—American, French, Eastern European —no longer rare gems, for they now exist in droves) set against the people in the grip of inertia. In my early youth, that opposition was an embarrassing experience, seemingly personal and peculiar to me alone, and it marked me, inclined me to proud isolation and to adopt the slogans of the political left; but now alienation is a badge of honor. However, I am not now what I once was, and although I can identify with my kindred spirits and share their anger, I am as well a bit mistrustful of their fiery anathemas.

Sacramento, a large city, and just another Desert Center spread over many square miles, has little appeal for me, and I would certainly not want to live there. It was there that a student, a young simpleton, asked me how life in Sacramento differed from life in a concentration camp. I had to assure him gently that there was a great difference, gently because even any persuasion would be lost on a person unable to distinguish between a pinprick and the rack. This young idiot had never faced starvation, he took a bath every day, drove a car, an old one but his own; he could take the works of Lenin and Mao Tse-tung from the library, and so he had forgotten what has first place in the hierarchy of human needs. He had forgotten, as well, how he had come to be where he was. For him the prosaic but tidy little houses, the palm-lined streets, the lawns, possessed the weight of things which exist in and of themselves. Even if he did sometimes imagine his part of that hot valley between the hilly coast and the foot of the Sierras in its former innocence—two hundred years back, more or less, when Johann August Sutter's fort alone stood there—it was only to grimace in contempt: was it worth it?

But, overall, auto trips about America result in admiration for man, and compassion. The enormity of this continent, its heaps of rocks, its sands, the dried salt-lake beds, all its hostile beauty leaves one, after a day's travel, with a certain sense of disconcerted triumph. For, after all, I could have been a man or a woman who crossed—after how many days or weeks?—the rocks and deserts I had seen, walking alongside an ox-drawn wagon or traveling on horseback. Ultimately, the value of anything on earth is measured by its resistance. Primeval, untouched nature is beautiful, but not to someone perishing of thirst or someone who, supported on a stick, drags a broken leg behind him. Though I see it with my own eyes, I cannot believe that people were able to master and tame this geological monster, tethering its body with ropes of highways, and what highways they are. The motel in a wild landscape of basalt blocks and yellow grasses has clean bedsheets, a comfortable bed, a bathroom with hot water. The waitress, the boy at the gas station in a little town surrounded by an area the size of Switzerland or Holland and inhabited by

rattlesnakes and coyotes, are as standardized as their
counterparts in the metropolis. But what if all this could
not have been achieved except at the cost of their minds?
Who would want to do what they do, be stuck where they
are? Not me. But, after all, they are toiling for me, instead
of me.

I am prepared to accept another aspect of automobile
travel with something like equanimity: the sight of man
destroying nature. From conquest to destruction? Where,
when, ought one to shout "Stop, enough." Northwestern
California was until quite recently a virgin redwood forest,
a wilderness of the oldest and largest trees in the world.
Today, to save what's left of them, the conservationists are
waging a war with the logging companies, a war none too
successful for the simple reason that the wood from one
such giant can make twenty houses. A lover of the forest, I
turn my eyes away from the hideous destruction on the
mountain slopes where the saws have passed. The ecologi-
cal balance destroyed, this forest will never grow back. Or
was that part of the cost, too? So people could work and
earn money in the sawmills, and so that something that the
maps call Arcata could be built near those sawmills? The
shores of San Francisco Bay were once tree-shaded, Indians once hunted wild fowl in its waters; camouflaging their
heads with leaves, the Indians would swim over to a flock
and grab a duck or wild goose by the leg. Now the hope of
profit requires that those shores be filled with garbage to extend the area usable for construction, and wastes from
factories are poisoning the water. Is this irrational and inevitable, or irrational and not inevitable? It is easy to see
that the automobile multiplies our questions because it
allows us to be ubiquitous.

On Virtue

*Appellata est enim ex viro virtus; viri autem propria
maxime est fortitudo.* [*The word virtue derives from* vir,
man, while courage best characterizes man.]

Cicero

Virtue, *virtus*, is that strength of character from whence
arise the qualities indispensable for standing up to the
world—courage, resolve, perseverance, control of the constantly changing emotions and impulses. If I regarded
nature sentimentally, I would treat virtue with less respect.
Since nature is not a loving mother but ravages and kills us
without qualms if we find ourselves in it without weapons
or tools, virtue must be held in high esteem, for it alone
permits the effective use of weapons and tools. The courage
(*fortitudo*) of which Cicero speaks may reside in the evil
and the good, the wise and the foolish. It manifests itself in
situations that exist independent of our will, and it commands us to behave in one definite way and no other.
Where the struggle with nature has imposed upon men the
necessity of organization, thus dividing them into those
who give orders and those who carry them out, the oppres-
sors and the oppressed, the master cannot dispense with

149

virtue without endangering his position as master, while the slave is compelled to virtue by his desire to survive and to outwit his master. The history of mankind is astonishing in its endless examples of virtue keeping societies, nations, and civilizations alive—the virtue of leaders and soldiers, torturers and the tortured, saints and criminals, captains and crews, owners and workers. No one can deny strength of character to Genghis Khan and his commanders, or to the knights of Cortes and Pizarro, or to the capitalist ascetics who tormented themselves as much as they did others, or to the generations of peasants who supported their families by hard labor on small plots of land. The human being is worthy of admiration because he suffers so much and remains undaunted in spite of it. If, for better or worse, our planet has been subjugated by technology, this probably did not occur because of some impersonal, inevitable laws of development, but because of the virtue of the groups, nations, and classes whose self-discipline created the appropriate conditions for it.

Until now, virtue had to be exercised in the struggle with nature and the struggle among men in which the losers met with extermination. Were it not for the abilities of self-discipline and self-denial, the conflicts that pitted men against each other would not have been so merciless. The greatest battlefields of our century—Verdun in World War I and the Russian plains in World War II—are enduring testimony to the unbelievable courage of the most ordinary men, the most anonymous country people and city dwellers who wore the uniform of the French and German, the German and Russian infantries. But, in times of peace as well, these same farmers, workers, shopkeepers, and bookkeepers gave proof of their merits, going to work each morning in acceptance of the rule "He who doesn't work doesn't eat." It was also their hands that made the cannon, machine guns, tanks, and shells with which they were to slaughter each other.

Arguments can be set forth against virtue, for it fosters obedience and is an agent of order, whatever sort that order may be, splendid or sordid. Heretics, renegades, and revolutionaries have not been devoid of virtue, but on the whole, virtue does not coexist very well with the anxious mind and the restless imagination. The mind, always somewhat skeptical, whispers its various doubts concerning our goals, even the smallest of them, when all our efforts should be directed toward their fulfillment; the imagination throws bridges from the present to the next hour or day, which is not healthy. Perhaps virtue leans toward the conservative or reactionary. One Polish critic reproached Joseph Conrad for glorifying the heroism of the crew in his tales of the sea. His seamen do not hesitate to sacrifice their lives to do what must be done, and they do not reflect on what is served by their efforts. The ship, however, is the property of the shipowners, who sent it to sea with a cargo of goods to be sold for a profit. Thus, Joseph Conrad is, indirectly, a defender of the established order; that is, capitalism. This conclusion is not entirely without its logic, especially since the poverty of the lower classes in Conrad's England was truly horrendous, but that logic is none too exacting, either. Any social system must appeal to the virtue of its workers, sailors, and soldiers or cease to exist. If, in the countries that are called socialist, the workers, sailors, and soldiers were to perform their duties out of love for the national economy, nobody would lift a finger. The critic's conclusion seems simply to mean that the virtue in people working for my affairs is praiseworthy, whereas it merits disapproval in those who work for my competitors and opponents.

There is no doubt, however, that a writer whose principal concern is the manly *fortitudo* of his heroes remains more or less insensitive to revolutionary slogans. The practice of virtue is difficult, it demands great willpower, and, for that reason, the hatred of one's superiors, the mocking of them and the goals they set, and the incitement of rebellion are rejected as dissension, anarchy, weakness, a temptation that must be overcome if one does not wish to be derelict in one's duty. The virtuous do not question. Whoever their captain, leader, or monarch may be, they do what they are told because they must. This does not mean that they are simply robots. They act in this way because others like themselves are beside them and they must be loyal to them, in solidarity with them. This solidarity can also be called conformism.

The United States is a land of virtue. Through virtue it arose and achieved its technical might. The solidarity of the colonists proved stronger than their loyalty to the English king; here one should ponder how and when virtue, though basically indisposed to mutterings and seditious acrimony, gives itself, once past a certain threshold, into the service of revolution. But those were not simple decisions, and both sides displayed great fortitude in the War for Independence, just as both sides did later on in the Civil War, an especially bloody conflict for the nineteenth century. But is not the entire growth of America the quest for profit, the worship of the golden calf, the rule of the dollar?

Undoubtedly. And is not money a quantitative standard of measure in the duels of men; is it not admitted that, empirically, the "best" man wins? Does not "best" mean the braver, the more competent, the more tenacious, the more industrious? And, above all, the one better able to repress his own momentary whims, fears, dreams, despair, cravings? Here virtue, unfortunately, seems to consist primarily of repression and renunciation. I would like to lie in the sun, but I get up and go because I must. I am afraid, but I forbid myself fear. I do not believe that what I am doing has any meaning, but I forbid myself to think that. I have worked enough, now I should take a rest, but I do not because I have, in advance, designated the hour, or the year, when I will be free to rest.

Repression. In the name of satisfying a need tomorrow, I deny myself its satisfaction today. Virtue, too, takes that form. Instead of enjoying a day off from work, I hit on the idea of devoting the day to fashioning a tool that will make my work easier tomorrow. The next day it occurs to me that it is worth devoting many days off to the making of a tool that will permit the fashioning of other tools in a shorter time, and so on. A parable of humanity producing machines that produce other machines that produce other machines. Or, in relation to an individual fate, a parable of someone who has toiled for decades, suppressed all his own needs, saving his money to someday finally "enjoy life," and who then realizes that it is too late, for he no longer has any desires. Or, to return to the literature of the sea, which always depicts the crew, a miniature society, pitted against an element representing the universe, Herman Melville's novel, *Moby Dick*, furnishes another example: Captain Ahab, obsessed by the pursuit of the white whale that gives him neither rest nor respite. Perhaps Ahab was insane, but he had, in its highest form, the virtue that represses its possessor as well as others.

Technology is virtue condensed, consolidated in tangible forms. Although technological progress can be imagined in a world of universal brotherhood, kindness, and peace, nothing of the sort has happened yet; any invention we can name was realized under conditions of more or less open and active force, compulsion, exploitation, with severe sanctions imposed on weakness. The two faces of technology, one beneficent, one malevolent, have their counterpart in the two faces of virtue, one of which is death's helper. For that simple reason, virtue has no love for squabblers and skeptics. One of the most virtuous peoples, the Germans, brought to power a madman more dangerous than Captain Ahab, for he was not commanding a ship but a nation that was obedient to him to the end, to the final catastrophe.

American virtue, primarily that of rural America, is nourished on naïveté, ignorance, ordinary dullness. The course of nearly every election leads one to suppose there is nothing so foolish that it cannot be used as bait, if only it is American enough—that is, is not marked as a foreign import. It would simply be light-mindedness not to see the seeds of destruction here, of the whole country by a new civil war, or of the whole world. The protest of the other America, now many millions strong, takes the form of hatred for virtue, for it is virtue which compels one to join the "rat race," to accept the given, to achieve, act, strive, to conform to the morals of one's neighbor.

To negate virtue, one must oppose industry with idle-

ness, puritanical repression of urges with instant gratifica-
tion, tomorrow with today, alcohol with marijuana, mod-
eration in the display of emotion with shameless emotional-
ity, the isolation of the individual with the collective,
calculation with carelessness, sobriety with ecstasy, racism
with the blending of the races, obedience with political rebellion, stiff dignity with poetry, music, and dance. In the
background there is the permanent conviction that *we have
gone too far*, that virtue has taken us too far; hence the
readiness to smash machines, those guardians of the house
of bondage. Among the revolt's many ingredients, the
strongest is probably the dream of a return. The place of
honor is given to primitive man, who has none of civilization's repressions, is not ashamed of his instincts, whose
body rhythms are joined with those of nature. No one outside of America is aware how deeply the revolutionary
gospel has been influenced by a religious admiration for
nature and an obsessive guilt at its poisoning and pollution
by business and industry.

The works of three American writers—Thoreau, Whitman, and Melville—sketched out (leaving room to grow)
all the problems that torment their heirs. At a time when
progress and Western civilization were being paid homage,
Melville did not believe in the beneficial results of industry
and commerce, and he rejected the Christianity which was
then respected, sincerely or insincerely. The narrator of
Moby Dick is set between Captain Ahab, in whom the virtue
and madness of Western Christian man are fused, and the
Polynesian, Queequeg. Victory falls (posthumously) to the
latter, a pagan with no care for the morrow, who lives in an
eternal now, devoid of any ambition to prove his worth
here or in the hereafter, free of any impulse toward self-

repression. Besides, for Melville, Queequeg had a different sort of *fortitudo* from the virtue of white men—the (Oriental) dissolution of the individual in the cosmic flow, in the universal cycle turning life into death and death into life, so that everything is accepted and actions are performed almost impersonally through submission to the great rhythm.

Virtue in the Western sense is now not only exposed to the malice of today's imitators of Queequeg, it is also subject to erosion from within, for, ultimately, it needs a certain complex of conventional beliefs to ensure its safety from the subversive whisperings of the mind and imagination. Literature and film have sufficiently acquainted us with the "breakdown" of the respectable citizen, who always did what was expected of him, worked from/until, earned a living, and then suddenly—often as a result of meeting a demon woman—discovers the emptiness, the absurdity of his way of life. This is a character invented by vindictive writers hostile to virtue. But breakdowns, though in somewhat less violent form, are not limited to individuals. The invisible withering of Christianity and the pressure of the myths of advertising (primarily the sexual myth or the myth of the Islands of Happiness, where what is natural is good) cannot help but weaken Puritanical restraint. The myths of advertising are in themselves contradictory. They create needs in order to stimulate ceaseless competition, which requires self-repression. At the same time its philosophy, opposed to the concept of Original Sin, deprives discipline of its basis and elevates today above a temporal or posthumous tomorrow.

There is a large element of uncertainty here; no one can measure the extent of the erosion or judge how today's virtue differs from the virtue of a hundred years ago. I have attended country fairs—in Oregon, for example, in the little town of Myrtle Point, Coos County. In that agricultural valley—not really rural, since there's so much smoke from sawmills and paper mills in the air—changing beliefs and convictions have been completely absorbed by the normal course of life, repeated from generation to generation.

The parade down Main Street, the American flag, the beautiful horses of the sheriff and his men, decorated saddles inlaid with silver. A band wearing false noses and Tyrolean hats goes by in a truck. The pom-pom girls, their ages ranging from sixteen to six, the smallest ones struggling awkwardly with their batons, sticking out their tongues. Floats with goddesses of plenty representing Progress or the blessing of Pomona. Clubs, associations, lodges. The Lodges of the Temple of the Orient: shopkeepers with painted-on mustaches, dressed up as Oriental kings in broad silk galligaskins, turbans, and slippers with pointed toes, pipe fifes and pound drums. Again, beautiful horses ridden by the children of farm families, boys and girls, long-legged, lean, straight in the stirrups, the costumes always changing, for one group follows another, the Caballeros, the River Rangers, the Coos Rangers. The cars of candidates running for local office or the state senate: "Vote for." A dragon that stretches out its neck every few seconds and belches smoke, an advertisement for a bulldozer company. Trucks, each carrying one felled tree more than a meter in diameter—the drivers are those who took first place in the professional competition, an event that makes sense in this region of sawmills. Much regal beauty —the queens of the melon growers, of the fishermen, of the county, the town. They throw kisses, smiles. A few girls are dressed up as squaws. There is even one genuine Indian leading a team of sheep dogs. Then the annual exhibits— stalls of cows, horses, sheep, pigs, domestic fowl, ribbons for first place, second, and honorable mention.

All this is quite typical and could be found in hundreds of small towns and counties across America. For a revolutionary, this is nothing more than the dull, insipid life of yokels and provincial boors. I, however, have a wonderful time at country fairs and applaud them. The difference between us is that, for me, all the frameworks that permit the daily practice of virtue are very fragile, it is easy to destroy them, as I saw for myself while observing ideologically planned regimes at close range. Virtue: to be thirteen years old, jump up every day at dawn to feed, water, and brush your own horse, bullock, ram, to learn everything that could ensure victory in the livestock competition. The long-haired revolutionary, usually raised in a big city in a well-to-do family, has no idea that a few thoughtless edicts are enough to ruin agriculture and set the lives of farm children on a completely different course, not necessarily a better one.

However, it is perfectly probable that a great change is gradually occurring and that there will be increasingly less virtue, simply because a smaller number of virtuous people will ensure the efficient functioning of society as a whole. If machines are virtue consolidated in matter, they can replace the efforts of the human will, and their cybernetic brains will not have to battle emotions, which do not exist in metal hearts. With the exception of a relatively small number of administrators, the remainder of the citizenry will be liberated from the afflictions and the triumphs *fortitudo* provides. Perhaps, but there is one other possibility that should not be excluded: perverse history, in order to check humanity's too-rapid progress, could throw its temporary support to systems that idolize economic inefficiency and privation, where everyone labors feverishly from morning till night with paltry results.

The Dance of Death
and Human Inequality

The dance of death was a popular subject for the painters in the late Middle Ages and, at times, during the Baroque period as well. In that dance, representatives of all social classes and professions and of all life's phases from childhood to old age followed behind death, the leader of the dance. In the presence of the ultimate, serfs and beggars were the equals of popes and bishops, kings and princes. Nevertheless, no one, aside from the followers of revolutionary-religious plebeian heresies, questioned the inequality of men in their earthly pilgrimage, an inequality caused by their having been born peasants, burgers, nobles. Later, when people were universally acknowledged as equal, the theoretical acceptance of this watchword was not synonymous with fully living out its meaning. The monetary privilege of some, the wrongs done others, though everyone was supposed to be afforded equal protection under the law, created divisions whose shamefulness served only to reinforce them. My own example verifies this, for there is no question that I am the child of privilege in the modern sense of the word. My parents valued education and so sent me to school, but there was more to it than that, for in school I enjoyed privileges which many of my schoolmates did not. I was familiar with a large number of expressions and ideas unknown to the boys from worker or peasant homes, and without working hard, I learned to express myself correctly in speaking and in writing. Resources like those brought from home are important, as I was to observe later on, when my own sons went to school in France, one of the most conservative of countries, where children at the age of eleven are classified—some will go to the *lycée* and are immediately marked for the upper class, and others will prepare for the "lower" economic occupations. Practicing the first lines of their reader, *Nos ancêtres les Gaulois*, my sons, who, of course have not a single drop of Gallic blood, were unable to understand a word. However, in their ability to use the language they very rapidly surpassed their schoolmates in elementary school, for the most part the sons of workers and petty tradesmen, and their calling for a *lycée* career was immediately recognized by their teachers. Apart from their inborn abilities, no small role was played here by the books in their home and the three languages, Polish, English, and French, in which we conversed with friends.

I completed high school and college, which did not, however, save me from servitude. At one time the privileged classes knew no concern about their daily bread, but the protection assured by education does not extend that far. Diplomas liberate one from physical work on a farm or factory; they do not liberate one from eight hours at a desk, drafting table, or laboratory. So, to my distaste, I learned that life was split into time sold and free time: the former unreal, boring, burdensome; and latter real, interesting, rich—but, for the most part, that was an illusion, since weariness does not let you make use of your free time.

There is nothing more important, more basic than that split, and for the majority of people the necessity of selling their time is a defeat they accept with resignation, as they accept death, for what other choice is there? In this regard my own biography took an exceptional shape. I was very lucky, my own stubbornness helped, and besides, the most varied historical circumstances kept knocking me out of the saddle. The periods of my servitude and affluence were brief, while my periods of complete freedom and poverty were long. I earned money by writing, but mostly what I liked and when I liked. And even poverty was not too annoying, or permanent either, for my books did bring me some money. Today I have absolutely no regrets about my fate, and even after long reflection, I could not imagine a condition better than the one I have attained. For many years I have been the master of my time, and my life is not split in two. I do not mean that I do not work for a living. However, the duties of a university professor, a burden for many, are no burden for me; on the contrary, the hours I spend with my students are spent in conversation, communication with my fellow men, which is, after all, the same goal one has in writing.

I am aware of my privileges, since there is much wisdom to the maxim that "existence determines consciousness" (on the condition that one does not oversimplify things here); I admit the idea that my position—a high one, if not in wealth, then in freedom—has the power to assuage my anger, irony, and sarcasm, for which our earth supplies many, even too many reasons. The privileged have always known how to arrange matters so that, while discussing elevated ideas, they do not confess the simplest thing—

that their days are spent not in toil on the so-called culti-vation of the arts and sciences.

Do the poets and philosophers ardently proclaiming human equality really believe that the maid serving them their coffee, the baker, bus driver, and municipal sanitation worker are their equal? The more complicated poetry and philosophy became, the more they were entangled in the thicket created by language itself, so that they ceased to be accessible, not only to the illiterate or semi-literate, but even to those with a decent education if they did not have the requisite training. The innocent, the poor in spirit, were earmarked to till the fields, drive the trains and buses, bake the bread, work as salesmen, their equality signified only by the right to a fair wage and safety from the lawlessness of the mighty or of the state. Likewise, the educated, if they opted for the good life and not the higher, spiritual aspira-tions, were accorded the ranks they had merited. The old aristocratic order was replaced by a new division—the caste of priests, the caste of merchants and warriors, the caste of executives. A true and deep experience of the truth of human equality is a rare and difficult thing. Perhaps it begins with the realization that poetry and philosophy, even if they employ abstruse methods, are not operations of pure intellect done in the name of pure intellect, but are connected with the dance of death in which everyone takes part, and so they are, potentially at least, for everyone. Only then can the breakthrough Karl Marx achieved be appreciated. For Marx there existed a single human sub-stance, which had been divided by the exigencies of history into temporary, transient yet enduring, figures—the en-trepreneur, worker, intellectual, peasant. And it is only with the inception of socialism, pervading everywhere today by osmosis, that we can date a new, more fully developed concept of equality.

The Polish socialist Jan Wacław Machajski, for many years a prisoner in tsarist Siberia, was the first person to express misgivings about the fate of equality in the future, post-revolutionary society. His disquisitions, written in Russian, took book form in *The Mental Worker*, published in 1905 in Geneva under the pseudonym A. Wolski. No less caustic than his professional revolutionary comrades when it came to evaluating the entire history of oppression and exploitation, Machajski differed from them in denying that history, a cruel and severe mistress, could change its ways by itself, and he spoke out against the "implacable laws of development," which were supposed to lead to the perfect society. He suspected the revolutionary movement of being a ruse to which the new caste, which wanted power, had resorted, even if it had done so in good faith. This new caste of mental workers was dissatisfied with their dependence on the capitalists. Their goal was to expropriate the capital by using the masses, and then to seize control of the economic administration and make the workers labor for the good of the entire society, which was identified with the ruling caste. Machajski thus advised the workers to distrust the white-collar intellectual leaders and to create spontaneous organization from below—a more radical revolution, in which the workers took the economy into their own hands.

Machajski's predictions have, in general, proven true. However, the anti-democratic, hierarchic structure of the societies ruled by the Marxists has not, to date, been subjected to an analysis that would permit an answer to the question "Why did it happen that way?"—i.e., how much needs to be ascribed to the mistaken or unconsciously deceitful assumptions of doctrine, and how much to the fateful forces at work when the ownership of the means of production passes into the hands of the state? The workers' interests are at cross-purposes with those of administrators who immediately monpolize both political and economic power. Thus, it would be necessary, as many rebels in the countries of Eastern Europe desire, to take power from the bureaucrats and give it to the workers' councils. That would mean the politicization of the average citizen to an unprecedented degree, exceeding even what we know of Athenian democracy. The obstacles here are considerable, but they do not seem to derive from a lack of ability on the part of the workers, already quick-witted, sober thinkers, to make difficult decisions. The obstacles are no doubt built into the mechanism of both production and government, the control of which would require constant vigilance and a near-daily participation in conferences. Unfortunately, as the experience of our times indicates, collective administration only works in a few cases, because people have only enough energy and interest for a couple of weeks of revolutionary elation, after which the professionals, the bureaucrats, take over the onerous duty of making decisions. And how to control them so that they defend the workers' interests, and not those at the top of the governing apparatus, remains a mystery.

The "acceleration of history" is, however, a fact; some gigantic overflow, an inundation of the human substance, which is now felt to be a single substance, an event occurring on a global scale, is just beginning, and it will not quickly settle in new channels. Changes of these dimensions must occur slowly; if measured by the length of one human life, I can thus have no hope of seeing a world which has been ordered to some degree. It must suffice me that I have witnessed an unprecedented awakening of human aspirations. Those aspirations form an entire scale and stimulate upward movement. In the industrialized countries, on the lowest levels, there is an impetus to flee from the countryside to the city, then from physical work to any other sort, as long as it does not demand muscle power. Because that process does not always end in success, universal education can cause great bitterness and hatred ("I know as much as he does, so why him and not me?"). But, even on a somewhat higher level, there is by no means a shortage of bitterness and hatred, for the selling of one's time ceases to be seen as a necessity of the human condition, and hence the ever-increasing eagerness for the "creative" professions that unite work and play with the inescapable "Why him and not me?" At the same time, the majority of mankind, who live in the underdeveloped and poor countries (and it is a fact that the poor countries get poorer and the rich richer) have other troubles. There, death from hunger is an everyday reality, and earning a living, whatever the work, as long as it allows one to avoid starving to death, is a dream not often realized. And so there is something indecent in the aspirations of our insignificant portion of Earth's inhabitants.

It is not my fault that whatever I think about human equality now assumes very American forms. The precious aristocratic pattern is still quietly preserved in Europe. I am sufficiently sober to grant more virtues to the American high school than to the French *lycée*, though the former are mostly bad and the latter mostly good. Admission is open to everyone in the American high school, not only to a chosen few. Opportunities are not equal, because, for example, a black from the ghetto must assimilate concepts and customs foreign to him, and, for an Indian, the civilization they are trying to cram him into is both repulsive and simply incomprehensible. Nevertheless, the selection process, applied not in childhood but in late adolescence, is, for that very reason, less strict, and the splendid careers of figures who sprang from the poorest of families are still a reality. A near-universal secondary education, whatever its quality, indicates the contours of the future; i.e., it invites reflection about what will happen when the workday is further shortened and, finally, a significant number of people are, either voluntarily or compulsorily, excluded from the process of production. Schools, universities, research institutes are already the principal places where a citizen's time is spent, and they will be of greater significance in the "post-industrial society."

There is a word that is practically never used today because it has an offensive reputation—boredom. Anyone who is usually bored will never admit it but will eagerly grasp at assurances that he is alienated, an outcast, lonely, frustrated, and so forth. But boredom, also known as *taedium vitae*, the knowledge of maya, that is, the meaninglessness of everything, *Weltschmerz, mal du siècle*, is a powerful force and should not be treated lightly. At the beginning of this book I spoke about the disturbances caused in our imagination by the instability of space, and that, ultimately, is the source of boredom. The endless space fashioned by the imagination can be compared to the fabric of a tent, which is either taut or slack and flapping in the wind. God, as a central point to which all space could be related, makes the fabric taut. On a smaller scale, the dream that shifts our minds from today to tomorrow fulfills a similar function. Then the slack space surrounding us is projected into the future in the form of desire, and tautness is thereby produced—e.g., one day I will be in the city I now wish to visit, one day I will drive the car I now wish to own, one day I will live in a better society. If neither God nor earthly goods nor a collective enterprise provides directional tension, space is inert, directionless, and soon colorless as well. For that reason, as well, love is the only salvation in the literature of boredom and alienation; all space forms around the one person who takes the place of God.

The so-called hunger for knowledge has, it would seem, only modest virtues when it comes to preventing boredom. The new inequality that is beginning to become apparent does not stem from the fact that some people have ability and others are dull, some industrious and some lazy, for everybody can be taught to read and write and scrape through school one way or the other. This new inequality is based on the fact that only a very few people are able to live without being bored. To organize one's completely free time single-handedly requires a special creative ardor that directs the setting of goals and the imposition of self-discipline in order to draw closer to those goals day after day.

Perhaps it is not atomic weapons and interplanetary travel which are creating a new era for humanity, but psychedelic drugs as an omen of mass, democratic means against boredom. The generation that has begun to use them (borrowing the discovery from the Mexican Indians and the blacks) does not deserve contemptuous abuse and is much better than the gilded American youth of the roaring twenties, for example, though their antics do tempt us to use the Russian saying: "Having it too good drives them crazy." Here we are probably dealing with the first human group brought up amid the products of technology that are accepted as normal, everyday, purely utilitarian, attracting little attention because of their abundance. Besides, as a former avid reader of *Mad* magazine, which that entire generation read in their school years, I think it was no small thing to get a whopping daily dose of the cruel, surrealistic humor that technological civilization uses to ridicule itself. (In Europe, humor of that sort was, until recently, solely the private code of the bohemian artist.) Finally, I must add that the generation under discussion here is the television generation, reaping all the consequences this entails, which are significant even if one ignores McLuhan's too precarious and, in general, mistaken, notions. It is also the generation of pop art, an art difficult to comprehend without a two-fold, ambivalent attitude toward television commercials.

I will try to explain, as simply as possible, what I imagine the significance of psychedelic trips to be. They are, in my opinion, an attempt to invest actual space with value so that the creation of intentional space becomes unnecessary. That sounds abstruse, but I don't want to alarm anyone. By actual space I mean that which surrounds me at a given moment and which I take in with my five senses. By intentional space I mean that which dwells in my imagination and calls out to be pursued. This can be God (always taking into account the very nature of our minds, which are caught in nets of spatial relations), or Captain Ahab's white whale, or a collective historical goal (Plato's Repub-

169

lic, a more just society, national liberation, etc.). Probably, actual space has full value only when we are moving through it toward a destination (then the material is taut). However, chemical means can so alter what our five senses receive that the space which surrounds us becomes full, infinitely rich, self-sufficient, and just to dwell in its midst is equivalent to dwelling in the godhead, making for the synesthesia long dreamed of by artists; that is, images becoming sounds and sounds images. Music builds whole edifices in space, the most interesting things happen on the table between the ashtray and the glass, colors literally "ring." For a truly religious person (this assumes a certain capacity for mystical experiences and should not be confused with belonging to any particular religious group), this, more or less, is in fact reality at its most ordinary, at every moment upheld and illuminated by the presence of the Deity. "The Open Doors of Perception" provide surrogate mystical states even though the transcendental God is replaced by an immanent God identical with the world. In essence, chemistry is acting here against the Judeo-Christian tradition and in favor of the Oriental tradition.

This magical medicine has an ambiguous influence. It strips bare prohibitions, rules, and virtue; everything regulated by society now appears as the rags used by average people, slaves to the "rat race," to try to cover the disturbing, uncommunicative core of existence. The rebellion makes use of this, though it is not, however, itself goal-oriented but anarchic, goal-free. At the same time, the psychedelic rituals highlight certain of tomorrow's more ominous features. It only took three decades for Aldous Huxley's *Brave New World* (1932) to cease being a book about the future. Paradoxically, toward the end of his life,

Huxley promoted the chemical equivalents of peyote because of their beneficent effects on old people in allaying the fear of dying. Somewhat earlier than Huxley's novel, Stanisław Ignacy Witkiewicz's *Insatiability* (1930) described the states produced by taking Murti Bing pills, which are almost identical with LSD. In *Insatiability*, Murti Bing makes people indifferent to social bonds and the afflictions of history, which in turn facilitates the Chinese conquest of Europe. Of course, it is doubtful that the missionaries of the chemico-mystical gospel are at present being discreetly financed by the Chinese, who ought to be eager for a slackening of virtue in America. Nevertheless, unusual opportunities are arising here for politicians of every stripe and ideology.

Full human equality will come to pass, but that may well be the equality of the subjected. People will be guaranteed bliss, but on condition that they do not interfere with the processes of government. Perfected chemical means will allow everyone to live each day in the midst of divine space. But other drugs that increase the ability to master knowledge and perform logical operations will be available only to a carefully selected few, members of the administrative caste. For the time being, that neat balance sheet is spoiled by injustice, poverty, hunger, and the unsatisfied aspirations of the majority of mankind. I recently came across a rather funny photograph in the newspaper. A young American in Nepal, long-haired, dressed in Oriental fashion, is surrounded by a dozen or so local boys with close-cropped heads, wearing European clothes, who are making fun of him. Even if he very much wished to, he would not be able to explain to them that the motorcycles and automobiles they long for are an illusion, the veil of maya.

171

Essay in Which the Author Confesses That He Is on the Side of Man, for Lack of Anything Better

I have often been asked why I, a poet, with a clear-cut vocation, engage in inanities; that is, write about things which can be grasped only in an improvised fashion, resisting precision. I, too, reproach myself for this and am consoled by the fact that, thus far, I have not written panegyrics in honor of any contemporary statesman—although more than once I have expended time on projects perhaps no less useless. But what I am doing now is not without function, at least for me. I am examining what is hidden behind my tendency to slip into social themes.

The world, existence, may be conceived as a tragedy, but, unfortunately, that view is no longer our specialty. Tragedy is grave, hieratic, while today we are assailed at every moment by monstrous humor, grotesque crime, macabre virtue. The dismal antics in which we all, willingly or not, have taken part (for these antics were History with a capital H) seemed to enjoin us to sprinkle our heads with ashes and weep like Job—but our Job shook with laughter for his own fate and, at the same time, for the fate of others. Every television switched on, every newspaper taken in hand evokes pity and terror, but a derisive pity, a derisive terror. I am no exception: while sympathizing with the victims of terror, I cannot control the sarcastic spasms wrenching my face when, for example, I learn that the police of a certain totalitarian state have made a series of arrests disguised as doctors and hospital attendants, having also painted their police cars with red crosses to look like ambulances. Those arrested were beaten unconscious, then carried off on stretchers by the "attendants." As has already been observed many times, reality's nightmarish incongruence has outstripped the boldest fantasies of the satirists. The entire style of my century is an attempt to keep pace with this depressing and ridiculous abomination, and can be felt in drawings, paintings, theater, poetry, the style of the absurd, and in our fierce and bitter jeering at ourselves and the human condition.

This style unites everything: the solitude of man in the universe, his imagination disinherited from a space related to God; images of what is taking place on the surface of the entire planet, which are constantly bombarding us; the neo-Manichaean hatred for matter; Promethean defiance in the name of human suffering is sent into a void, since there is no addressee. This medley of ingredients makes for an ambivalent style, and nearly every work can be interpreted with equal validity either as metaphysical despair or as a curse hurled at man's cruelty to man, at evil society.

I do not like the style of the absurd and do not wish to pay it homage by using it, even if I am assured that it derives from protest. Black gallows humor is too much an admission of complete impotence; mockery has long been the only revenge for the humiliated, the oppressed, slaves. Although today's sensibility is so blunted that, without the stimulation of tricks from the Grand Guignol, our voice is heard by practically no one, contempt for fashion has, on the whole, kept me from making concessions. Possibly my need for order is exceptionally great, or perhaps I am classical in my tastes, or perhaps mine are the ways of a polite, naïve boy who received a Catholic upbringing. I think, however, that in my need for order, my reluctance to grimace hellishly in response to the absurd, I am quite average, except that I am less ashamed of my heart's demands than other people.

I do not like the style of the absurd, but neither do I like the natural order, which means submission to blind necessity, to the force of gravity, all that which is opposed to meaning and thus offends my mind. As a creature of flesh, I am part of that order, but it is without my consent. And with absolute sobriety I maintain that although today our imagination cannot deal with a division of existence into the three zones of Heaven, Earth, and Hell, such a division is inevitable. Man is inwardly contradictory because he resides in between. For me, the talk of some Catholics—wishing to buy their way into the good graces of the unbelievers—about the goodness of the world, is no more than a fairy tale. On the contrary, I do agree with Simone Weil when she says that the devil does not bear the title Prince of This World in vain. Certainly, the causes and effects that govern matter with mathematical necessity do not entitle us to hurl abuse at God or at any X designating the very basis of existence. If we can leave our humanity aside for a moment and put our human sense of values out of mind, we must admit that the world is neither good nor evil, that such categories do not apply to the life of a butterfly or a crab. It is, however, another matter when we are dealing with our own demands, demands peculiar to us amid everything alive. Then indifferent determinism assumes diabolical features and we have the right to suppose that God has leased the universe to the devil, who, in the book of Job, is one of Jehovah's sons. "The war we wage with the world, the flesh, and the devil" is not a contrivance of Spanish mystics but occurs within us and as well between us and the indifferent necessity surrounding us. I am two-fold: to the degree that I am the kin of the butterfly and the crab, I am the servant of the Spirit of the Earth, who is not good. If there were no man, there would be no devil, for the natural order would not have been contradicted by anyone. Since it is contradicted, its ruler, Satan, the Spirit of the Earth, the demiurge of nature, battles with what is divine in man for the human soul. And only the covenant with God allows man to disengage himself, or rather to attempt to disengage himself, from the net of immutable laws binding creation.

I am, thus, frankly pessimistic in appraising life, for it is chiefly composed of pain and the fear of death, and it seems to me that a man who has succeeded in living a day without physical suffering should consider himself perfectly happy. The Prince of This World is also the Prince of Lies and the Prince of Darkness. The old Iranian myths about the struggle of Darkness with Light, Ahriman against Ormazd, suit me perfectly. What, then, is the light? The divine in man turning against the natural in him—in other words, intelligence dissenting from "meaninglessness," searching for meaning, grafted onto darkness like a noble shoot onto a wild tree, growing greater and stronger only in and through man.

Consciousness, intelligence, light, grace, the love of the

good—such subtle distinctions are not my concern; for me
it is enough that we have some faculty that makes us alien,
intruders in the world, solitary creatures unable to communicate with crabs, birds, animals. According to an old
legend common in the first centuries of Christianity and
later forgotten, Satan revolted because God ordered him,
the firstborn, to pay homage to man, who had been created
in God's likeness and image. From then on, all Satan's
activities have had a single aim—to rival the younger
brother so unjustly exalted. Or, to offer a somewhat different reading, enmity was established between us and nature.

We are unable to live nakedly. We must constantly wrap
ourselves in a cocoon of mental constructs, our changing
styles of philosophy, poetry, art. We invest meaning in that
which is opposed to meaning; that ceaseless labor, that
spinning is the most purely human of our activities. For the
threads spun by our ancestors do not perish, they are preserved; we alone among living creatures have a history, we
move in a gigantic labyrinth where the present and the past
are interwoven. That labyrinth protects and consoles us,
for it is anti-nature. Death is a humiliation because it tears
us away from words, the sounds of music, configurations of
line and color, away from all the manifestations of our anti-
natural freedom, and puts us under the sway of necessity,
relegates us to the kingdom of inertia, senseless birth, and
senseless decay.

Yes, but the absurdity that afflicts us today is, first and
foremost, the work of man. Civilization does not satisfy our
desire for order, for clear, transparent structure, for justice,
and finally, for what we instinctively apprehend as the fit-
ness of things. The savagery of the struggle for existence is
not averted in civilization. Opaque, automatic, subordinate

to the most primitive determinants, and subordinating us so much that it levels and grinds us down, civilization does not approach but rather recedes from the models of a republic at long last fit for man, as postulated by philosophers for more than two millennia. That happens because the duality residing in each of us is in fact sharpened by civilization. The devil brilliantly exploits technology in order to penetrate to the interior of our fortress and manipulate our mechanisms; that is, the determinism and inertia of what is not human drags what is divine in man down as well.

For many of my contemporaries, the devil is the inventive, coldly logical mind, as well as the creator of the technological civilization by which we are increasingly elevated and oppressed. For that reason, many people side with the instincts and intuition of natural, individual man against the artificial and the collective. It is also true that in the popular imagination the self-confident know-it-all with his books, reducing everything to the mechanisms of cause and effect—dry, devoid of faith, indifferent to good and evil—has often been synonymous with the evil spirit. This image is maintained by the comics, film, and television, where the villain, a criminal in a white lab coat, is made omnipotent by his laboratory. For me, however, the responsibility for our misfortunes is not borne by intellect but by intellect unenlightened, insufficiently rational, cutting itself off from those gifts of ours—grace or attachment to value, by whatever name—from which it should be inseparable. I am no friend of the rationalists, either those of the eighteenth century or their successors. But if today's opponents of impersonal, repressive, inhuman knowledge are quick to cite William Blake, I am with them only because I find in Blake something different than they do. The intellect that oppressed Blake renounced impulse in favor of the fixed laws of matter, and renounced ascending movement in favor of inertia. Newton's physics horrified Blake because he saw them as a declaration of subjection, our subjection to what is; since things are as they are, there is no choice in the matter.

In modern times the great metaphysical operation has been the attempt to invest history with meaning. That is, we, as foreigners, intruders, face a world that knows neither good nor evil; our divinity is weak, imprisoned in flesh, subject to time and death; so let our labyrinth but increase, let our law, born of the challenge we hurl at the world in the name of what should be, be established. Our existence, like that of crabs and butterflies, does not lend itself to deliberations on its own purpose, all our *what fors* and *whys* fall away; meaning can only be made from what resists meaning if, from one generation to the next, there is an increase in the purely human need for justice and order, which also permits us to postulate the moment when humanity will be fulfilled. Curious dislocations and substitutions have occurred in the course of that attempt. God changed into a malevolent, cruel demiurge, the tyrant Zeus, the tyrant Jehovah, because he was the god of nature, which contradicts and dissatisfies us; many people have opposed that god with a divine hero, a leader of men, namely, the rebel Prometheus, Lucifer (who often had the face of Christ), as did the Romantic poets. Later, anyone who wished to see history in motion and directed toward a goal was required to express himself in the language of atheism. However, the change did not relieve this process of any of the traditional violence that occurs whenever ultimate concerns are at stake.

This much should be said lest I be suspected of possessing the instincts of an activist, which are, in fact, rather weak in me. The social and the political are forced onto us, since we have no defense against time and destruction outside of them. The labyrinth spun by the generations is so truly splendid, so interesting, that just to wander through it affords one much joy, and I do not blame people for never poking their noses from books or museums. And there is also the making of art, which is continually infusing human freedom with new life. But, upon closer examination, one sees that that entire humanistic space withers and dies if it's not stimulated by a reaching out from stagnant to new forms; while, by virtue of laws, which I shall not mention here, the new always allies itself with the social and the political, though sometimes in a highly roundabout way.

Our age has been justly called the age of new religious wars. That would make no sense if the Communist revolutions were not rooted in metaphysics; that is, had not been attempts to invest history with meaning through action. The liberation of man from subjection to the market is nothing but his liberation from the power of nature, because the market is an extension of the struggle for existence and nature's cruelty, in human society. The slogans used by the two camps, the adherents of the market and the revolutionaries, thus take on an aspect that is quite the reverse of what they seem at first sight. The enemies of revolution loved to appear as the defenders of a religion threatened by atheists, while those atheists hated them as the priests of an inferior god, Zeus, Jehovah, otherwise known as the devil, who tramples the divine impulses in man. This is the meaning of History which Marxism opposed to Nature. Marxism is thus in harmony with the neo-

Manichaean ferocity of modern man. Were it not, it would not exercise the near-magical attraction it has for the most active minds and would not be a central concern for philosophers.

Only when a metaphysical core is recognized in what seems to be merely social and political can the dimensions of the catastrophe that has befallen us be assessed. Hopeful thought moved into action and returned to thought, but now bereft of hope. The collapse of faith in the meaning of history as a result of the revolution which was both victorious and a failure concerns, to be sure, only Europe and North America, but we must have the nerve to admit that we neither can nor very much desire to share the hopes of Asians, Africans, and Latin Americans, for we assume tacitly, and perhaps quite wrongly, that there will be a repetition of a pattern with which we are already familiar.

It is easy to miss the essence of revolutionary intention, for it is usually obscured by sentimental and moralistic slogans. It is also easy to argue that what happened had to have happened. Marxism wanted to act against the devil but let him in through a loophole in doctrine. That is, because of its scientific ambitions, Marxism glorified necessity, which supposedly was to be the midwife of men's freedom. In this manner, terror acquired the sanction of a *Weltgeist* invested with all the trappings of an evil demiurge. This was none too friendly a blessing for any better tomorrow. And thus, in the countries ruled by Marxists, the Prince of Lies put on a performance that made all his previous exploits pale by comparison. However, it should not be forgotten that, in retrospect, we are always inclined to ascribe to events more developmental logic than they in fact possessed.

What is the trap we are caught in today? My childhood was marked by two sets of events whose significance I see as more than social or political. One was the revolution in Russia, with all its various consequences. The other was the omen of Americanization, the films of Buster Keaton and Mary Pickford, the Ford motorcar. Now there is no doubt that Americanization has carried off complete victory: Americanization means the product of forces not only lower than man and not only outstripping him, submerging him, but, what is more important, sensed by man as both lower than and outstripping his will. Who knows, perhaps this is a punishment for man's claims on the forbidden. The more God abandoned space, the stronger became the dream of building the Kingdom of God here and now with our own hands, which, however, condemned man to a life of getting and spending. Fine, why should it be any other way? The only question is whether our two-fold nature can endure a static reality, and whether we, if forbidden to reach out beyond that reality and beyond our nature, will not go mad, or, to use the language of psychiatrists, succumb to an excess of "problems." It may well be that we are healthy only when trying to leap from our own skins, in the hope of succeeding from time to time.

Something important, at least to me, emerges from what I have said. There seems to be much truth in what I have read in histories of religion about the circle symbolizing Greek thought. A circle has neither beginning nor end, on its circumference "was" flows into "is" and returns to "was." The exact opposite holds for Jewish thought, which is well depicted by the sign of the arrow. The flight of that arrow: the Covenant with God, the journey of the chosen people through the ages, the promise of a Messiah. This was inherited by Christianity, and it is the source of secular messianic dreams as well. Even the prosaic bourgeois concept of progress in the second half of the nineteenth century occasioned expectations that seem comical to us today, as can be seen in Bolesław Prus's novel *The Doll*, where the invention of a metal lighter than air was to assure universal peace and universal happiness. For me these are very personal matters. The education I received set me forever under the sign of the arrow, an education not confined to school. Yet in America, where I live, in this phase of civilization, every man must somehow cope with his situation—that of a fly trapped in amber. He is surrounded by that which has lost its ability to maintain direction and has begun to take on a circular form. Interplanetary voyages hold little promise of our entering another human dimension, and probably only the legend of flying saucers provides any outlet for our yearning for something completely other, through contact with little green men arriving here from some distant planet. The mind either behaves perversely, delighting in visions of destruction, catastrophe, apocalypse (in this respect, American intellectuals are reminiscent of their European colleagues of the twenties and thirties), or consoles itself with an eternally recurrent cosmic harmony in disharmony. Perhaps the circle is not an exact representation of Greek thought on time-space, but some kinship between Greece and India, and the present interest in Oriental wisdom, may be a result of the restraints imposed upon our images of ascending movement.

In any case, America, by virtue of its entire development, whose driving force was automatic, unplanned movement, has always suffered from a certain weakness in historical imagination—yesterday and tomorrow are like today, a little worse, a little better, which is perhaps why in American films both ancient Romans and astronauts from the year 3000 look and act like boys from Kentucky. The imagination had a naturalistic orientation—man, eternally the same, eternally in the power of the same drives and needs, faced a nature also eternally the same. Commercial advertising fell into this pattern easily and contributed to its reinforcement. Advertising appeals to the physiological sides of what is "eternally human": sex; the ingestion of food (appetizing dishes which make your mouth water); excretion (pills regulating the stomach, toilet paper delightful to the touch); ugly odors (mouth washes, deodorants).

I am ill-disposed to the philosophical propositions that current literature, art, and advertising offer me. Every man and woman I pass on the street feels trapped by the boundaries of their skin, but, in fact, they are delicate receiving instruments whose spirituality and corporality vibrate in one specific manner because they have been set at one specific pitch. Each of them bears within himself a multitude of souls and, I maintain, of bodies as well, but only one soul and one body are at their disposal, the others remaining unliberated. By changing civilizations, time continually liberates new souls and bodies in man, and thus time is not a serpent devouring its own tail, though ordinary men and women do not know this. Once, a very long time ago, walking down the street in a Polish village, I grew thoughtful at the sight of ducks splashing about in a miserable puddle. I was struck because nearby there was a lovely stream flowing through an alder wood. "Why don't they go over to the stream?" I asked an old peasant sitting on a bench in front of his hut. He answered: "Bah, if only they knew!"

The Rebirth of Utopia:
Herbert Marcuse

> *The quantification of nature, which led to its explication in terms of mathematical structures, separated reality from all inherent ends and, consequently, separated the true from the good, science from ethics. . . . Then the precarious ontological link between Logos and Eros is broken, and scientific rationality emerges as essentially neutral.*
>
> Herbert Marcuse, *One-Dimensional Man*

The writings of Herbert Marcuse, for a while my colleague at the University of California, have enjoyed a great response among students because even animals, if sick, will eat medicinal plants. Marcuse brings them tidings that man is rational and only his collective creation, which he has let engulf him, is irrational. It is irrational because the blind brutality inherent in daily life has not been warded off by our divine-human aspirations; on the contrary, by relating to it neutrally, we have become reconciled to that brutality. The scientific mind indifferent to good and evil—Logos cut off from Eros—is at the basis of what man has created collectively. Marcuse's apprehension of Eros is Platonic. In Dante there is the "Love that moves the sun and other stars." The "Reason" Marcuse combats is a "bandit who

buys arms," a demonic scientist in a white lab coat straight
from the comic books. William Blake combats the diabolic
vassal of inertia responsible for the inhuman industrializa-
tion of England, or, as Allen Ginsberg calls it, "Moloch
whose name is the Mind."

Reason guided by Eros establishes universal ideas which,
by the very fact of their existence, contradict what *is* in the
name of what *should be*. Man, barely a sketch, an outline
of himself, strives to incarnate them in life; that is, to tear
himself from the bonds of what is allegedly irreversible
necessity. Time is on his side. For it is not true that "there
is nothing new under the sun." Universal ideas are constantly being projected into the future and lead toward the
victory of what is divine and human in man. Time is not
circular.

There is nothing more typical of America, which first
exploited the immigrations of unskilled workers, then the
"immigration of talents," than an import like Marcuse.
What is thought-provoking here is that Marcuse, a Marxist
of German extraction, by a certain clarification of chaos,
especially by a defense of reason, which is not for him
identical with Moloch, provides American youth with a
scrap of hope. In keeping with the general crisis in
Promethean faith, he also must be a disinherited Marxist,
one who saw Marxism defeated in Europe in both its revolutionary and its evolutionary forms. The Marxists' ambition to construct a "scientific world view" brought them
close to the devotees of Logos, who were inclined to dispense with Eros. According to their doctrine, the developmental laws of matter, by "implacable necessity," had to
lead to a redemptive revolution brought about by the pre-
destined class, the working class. Recent decades have not

been entirely kind to these proud scientific calculations. Or else the result was simply in keeping with those calculations, since necessity had given birth to a bureaucratic state founded on terror as a permanent and inevitable institution. For tigers usually give birth to tigers. In Marcuse there is, thus, no prediction of inevitable revolution, inevitable because it, in some sense, already pre-exists in the relations of production. Those relations of production are able to manage perfectly well without a fundamental revolution, and universal well-being lies within the reach of their powers. So much so that one can state only that reason will not endure constant violation by unreason, and that collective unreason is an outgrowth of the existing relations of production. Thus, a revolution is barely a postulate; there is no guarantee of it besides the assumption that, in spite of numerous defeats, the final victory belongs to an ever-more enlightened Reason. To the objection that such an assumption does not have a leg to stand on, Marcuse would undoubtedly reply that we are unable to stop at relative half-truths, since we are seeking absolute truth. That refers us to the most fundamental questions about the structure of the universe and to belief or disbelief in its hidden intelligent principle, which man, alone among all living creatures, helps to create. Marcuse finds no Messiah able to lead man to the Promised Land, for, after all, conservative American workers are not a very good bet. He is counting on new arrangements of forces within the whirl of chaos, as well as on events difficult to foresee.

I don't know how Marcuse is read in Europe. His abstractions enjoy a special power in America, and his success with the young is no mystery. It is very difficult to live feeling that reality is covered by a veil or multitude of veils that one tries to draw aside in order to get at something "firm"—but the veils are invisible, moving, slippery; they elude names because their perversity is so great they are transformed as often as they are named. Comedy and terror flow over them in waves of images of the absurd. Under such conditions, not far from schizophrenia (one of whose symptoms is that a schizophrenic may see a tree but it is not completely real; a real tree is expected to appear any moment, but it never quite does), Marcuse comes forth and says: This happened because you are unfree. The tyranny oppressing you does not have any command center in any palace or castle, no one has planned it and it need not resort to orders and prohibitions. But the control which is exercised over you is total, for you have been transformed from within—your mind, your emotions, your desires do not belong to you, they have been imposed by society's rituals. If you want to be free, the first step must be the realization that any of your reflections on daily life, on man, are not independent, since the material at your disposal, the material of your perceptions and ideas, is not your own as you believe. It is not with the world that you are communicating but with your own civilization, which disguises itself and passes itself off as the world. So let consciousness discover how and by what means you are manipulated. That can be done.

The instrument of control employed by the collective is language—spoken, written, pictorial. The information that language transmits can be evaluated with relative ease, but the dislocations of meaning brought about in language by the elimination of certain expressions, the inverting of concepts, even through syntax, are much more difficult to perceive. Marcuse considers the analysis of language to be the principal task, although he seems not to have any doubts about the somewhat daunting dimensions of such an enterprise. He attacks language that breaks the reality we perceive into fragments of "facts," since that language fully supports a cow-like view of the world—we don't know what a cow staring at a passing automobile thinks, but we sense that it is something on the order of a pure statement: it's there, nothing more than that. According to Marcuse, there is a close connection between the colloquial language that fashions everyone imperceptibly and the limitations of the philosophers it has also fashioned. To the delight of his young readers, Marcuse concentrates his attack on positivist philosophy, powerful in American universities, and especially despised by the students. For that philosophy renders any longing for a coherent world view impossible and derides that longing as well. "Values detached from objective reality become subjective," to use Marcuse's words, and what is subjective is not considered philosophical. The young turn away from such linguistic games, which they find sterile—a healthy impulse on their part, for what sort of philosophy would investigate a valueless, cow-like world? But they are then condemned to dangle in the void of their own subjectivity, an all-consuming relativism from which neither hallucinogens nor Eastern religions will save them. According to Marcuse, however, positivist philosophy is not an innocent exercise practiced by armchair sages. In agreement with science in a common contempt for Eros—values, detached and banished—it strives to perfect the language of technological domination.

Marcuse's writings have helped a number of people regain self-respect. To feel helpless before the efficiently functioning organism one inhabits leads to the shifting of all responsibility for one's personal setbacks onto that organism and to paralysis of the will. Dostoevsky in his *Diary of a Writer* noted a similar tendency among the Russian intelligentsia, who did not recognize individual guilt, holding the environment responsible instead. Dostoevsky saw this as the renunciation of Christianity by the intelligentsia. Besides, it was not only in Russia that progressives of various persuasions railed at the moralists: man is evil because the system is evil, change the system and you change man. In the currently fashionable afterdinner conversations about alienation, man's lost essence, which could be regained were it not for external conditions, is almost identical with the inborn goodness of the noble savage before he had been brought down by society. This tendency is even stronger in America because of its long-standing cult of the primitive. Natives from the islands of Polynesia, Indians, blacks, have always been seen here as a promise of some forbidden freedom, offering some vague, alluring world of possible return to nature and fraternization (often with a hint of homosexuality). And so the popular slogan among the young, "Drop out," has a twofold meaning—both a flight into the natural (reducing needs, not cutting the hair, not washing, nakedness, group sex) and political rebellion. However, although Marcuse and other writers with a Marxist orientation are comforting because they confirm one's innocence, their books authorize no conclusions about the existence, here and now, of some good human essence that need only be uncovered like a bouquet of flowers wrapped in hideous newspaper. Quite the contrary, for them man is what he is not; his essence is aspiration and unfulfillment. That is very alien to the primitivist fantasy, very European, in spite of Europe's tendency to interweave the two nostalgias, for the past and for the future (cf. the works of Romanticism). Probably primeval innocence is so attractive to young Americans because it serves the interests of a commercial civilization that has rejected Original Sin, and so they are more that civilization's legitimate children than they might think.

Marcuse satisfies certain of my early acquired habits; he is from the tradition in which I was raised. That tradition provided me with the conviction that the key to the human condition lay in the marriage of Logos and Eros. Nevertheless, I find a bit too much contradiction in Marcuse. Since we negate that which *is* because reality is still equated with the state of nature (nature shifted onto society), we then desire to imagine that which *should be*. "No" would be Marcuse's reply, we can do more than behave like pure negativity. Because what exists has such great weight that it encloses us from all sides in a charmed circle of common sense. Thinking soberly, we encounter no information able to convince us that things could be other than they are. The possible is not desired, but what is desired seems impossible. If we reflect on technology, economics, politics, we grow enmeshed in a series of interdependent systems and come to the conclusion that dehumanization is inevitable. Arguments against the ideal republic of goodness and kindness will be irrefutable since the scope of our argument has been constricted to what *is*. Thus, it is not difficult to discover the entire Marxist legacy in Marcuse. Capitalist relations of production have, according to Marx, so contaminated the mind in its striving to revolt, that it is capable only of negativity. Only by abolishing those relations of production can the mind be liberated. For that reason as well, Marx gives almost no indication of how to organize the post-revolutionary state, a lapse which has had no little consequence. But Marx at least placed his hopes in a Messiah, the working class, pure negativity as a class. Marcuse's Marxism has been dispossessed of its Messiah. His young readers can thus neither strive to change existing institutions (for that will always be no more than a partial change not affecting the very root of dehumanization) nor count on a Messiah who will triumph because he must triumph. Marcuse's teachings are thus in keeping with the mass student revolt, which knows what it doesn't want but doesn't know what it wants.

As with many Marxists, hatred for man as he is in the name of man as he ought to be determines the emotional tone of Marcuse's writings. Even if we accept man as a nearly infinite potentiality, while measuring the distance between his achievements that occur from time to time and his actual limitations today, such hatred disposes us to suspicion, for it is unjustified unless we can draw a line where ideal man begins. But if that line is to be drawn by a rather problematic revolution that will provide the solution to everything, then Marcuse's philosophical premises are overthrown. The mind never ceases transcending itself and is always pursuing the receding heaven of the idea; and the body, the abode of Eros, the god of all the creative impulses, never escapes the necessity of physiology. Thus, man as he is, here and now, who lives out his modest segment of time and who will not, after all, have any other, ought at least to have our compassion even if he doesn't inspire us to active brotherhood. To consider the citizens of any country, as Marcuse does, depraved creatures, blameless idiots but idiots nonetheless, is to condemn oneself to intellectual arrogance. In America, that means treating all technology as something that exists, complete and self-evident, and to reflect only on its ominous consequences. Technology, however, was not born from nothing. It recapitulates all the savagery, all the ruthlessness of the struggle for survival, and contains enormous human virtue as well. Does it matter if technology is just condensed savagery? One must always remember how it has revealed itself to peoples held in contempt—the slaughtering of entire tribes, giving them blankets infected with smallpox, slavery both manifest and half hidden. But what to do, if this is the infamous background of its beneficent gifts? No one of any consciousness will call for destruction of the machines, and neither does Marcuse. It is one thing to concede at least reluctantly that (capitalist) machines have lifted the human masses above the level of naked survival, and quite another not to take any particular machine for granted. For that reason, the average American, despised by Marcuse, values the use of machines and is grateful to the system which gave them to him, since he remembers that his father or grandfather once lived in a one-room hut along with the cow and the goat. No doubt that man is Marcuse's enemy, for man wants no changes that threaten to take away what he has, and he will support the politicians who play on his fear of the unknown.

The European knows this conflict by heart. In Europe, pure, sensitive, thinking people turned against the inert masses who had to be saved even if it were against their will. If a person does not wish to be what he ought to be, he must be hoisted by terror. This culminated in the doctrine of the dictatorship of the proletariat, and thus, in theory, the dictatorship of the majority over the minority, and, in practice, the minority over the majority. The bloody battles

of American workers for bread, for the right to have trade
unions, the right to strike, did not have such a philosophical character. Now, however, it is difficult to transplant
Marxist ideas to American soil, for it is not possible to
deceive oneself that the young and a proletariat isolated by
skin color could have the majority on their side.

Marcuse, in spite of his unavoidable contradictions, represents a clarification, and one really wishes that he were
read by the rebels who simply engage in hatred. But,
for the most part, they are not interested in theory. Or
history. The bits of theoretical equations they do need, they
get by touching each other's antennae like ants. Those
equations can be reduced to: "We live in the absurd, the
absurd should be destroyed." The first half of the twentieth
century seems far away to them; they were children then or
not yet born. They do not consider history the teacher of
life, and besides, they were never acquainted with it in
school. Theirs is an irrational impulse (they ridicule anyone who tells them that's bad), their voluntarism is blind
(what's wrong with its being blind?). Their goal is not a
new system (what sort?) but revolutionary action (political action painting?). Their "let it be" means "let the destruction be." Are they in need of work, money, bread?
Hardly. Their moralistic impulses are strong, but something other than morality has been catalyzed by the war in
Vietnam. As with the Russian nihilists, their desire for a
general conflagration is the final link in a self-begetting
chain. They also recall the Russian nihilists by the way they
exclude themselves from the mass of their own people,
whom they view as benighted, and thus a burden.

The destruction they desire does not seem a chimerical
goal to them, for the more technology, the more delicate are

the nerves of the Leviathan whose most sensitive points they wish to stab. To provoke it so that it will respond with blows and reveal itself as physical violence does not contradict their intentions, because they assume that democracy is a delusion supported by the ignorant majority. It is possible that, without knowing it, they are a tool in the hands of the sly spirit of history, which is still a mystery to us. It is more likely that the collective body they are attacking secreted them like a toxin in order to dissolve and assimilate them, keeping itself vital by continually digesting new doses of radicalism.

California has frequent earthquakes, though they are barely strong enough to feel. Geologists are predicting an earthquake as major as the one that destroyed San Francisco in 1906. It could happen in a month, a year, or in fifty years—for dislocations in the earth's crust, those are small differences. One could either see a recklessness in building on the fault, the deepest on the continent, which runs right beneath the towns by the Bay, or recognize the educational virtues of such stubbornness: if our fragility and our transience expose us to forces beyond our control, why worry too much? Similarly, American democracy, guaranteeing its citizens the right to subversive propaganda, has, right from the beginning, lived in a state of permanent crisis, forcing itself to somersault from one day to the next. Only at the high cost of a war between the North and the South did the conglomeration of independent states prevail as one nation. The durability of this republic of fugitives, durability through being provisional (for its existence, as in the Arabian fairy tale, had released a genie that had to be dealt with in order to liberate new genies in turn), is very modern; it corresponds to our new habits based on the knowledge that not only civilizations are mortal but all humanity as well. Perhaps so-called primitive man was happy because danger came to him from without, from hostile nature, which he entreated with magical dances. But he is not worth envying. The sight of his remains, the bones found in Tuzigoot, Arizona, for example, caused me a moment of pity. In that era the average human life did not exceed thirty years. It is hard for me to comprehend how our species endured to the present, considering its alienness and the omnipotence of the demons opposing it. The monsters the species has harnessed to serve it extend our life span, but those monsters are also ready, in the form of technology or of collective suicidal mania, to relieve the earth of our presence, no doubt a fair enough bargain.

For me the human labyrinth is splendid, spellbinding. Besides, it matters little what I think of it; what I am in relation to it is important. Perhaps because, in spite of everything, I had a patriarchal childhood, I remain superstitious, something I cultivate. I believe that there is such a thing as exceeding the limit, and that every such action calls down an avenging verdict. Ever-increasing complication is both inevitable and desirable, but it is impossible to get by without some great purge, some great reduction every so often. I do not know how and by whom that will be accomplished, but I trust that my aversion for the contemporary style, which aims to reduce me to helplessness, like a spider does a fly, not only stems from my attachment to the past but is an acknowledgment of a principle opposing the lack of all restraint. And although ninety percent of what I am offered in books, films, and paintings strikes me as a loud and empty uproar, I do not imagine the great purge the way Herbert Marcuse does. Unlike him, I do not equate rage at necessity with the purity of protest against imperfect society. The mark of today's style is rage directed against Existence. Though there are many Manichaean elements in me, I find such rage indecent, and it is my guess that God does not like it either. Necessity can be overcome only by remembering that it will never be entirely overcome, and that the "limited empirical world," loathed and ridiculed by Marcuse, where, he says, "the broom in the corner and the taste of pineapple have great significance," will never cease to preoccupy us. There is no reason to gloat at the stupidity of average people because their horizons are narrowed by their daily work and pastimes, because they are not grieving every minute of the day and night over a world composed of "gas chambers and concentration camps, Hiroshima and Nagasaki, American Cadillacs and German Mercedes-Benzes, the Pentagon and the Kremlin, atomic cities and Chinese communes, Cuba, brainwashing, and massacres." But what about diseases, and worldwide epidemics, not to mention the universality of death? Changed into a politicized angel, man would burn with the most holy wrath against what *is* and, one may assume, would have all the makings of an inquisitor or a servant of the Inquisition.

You are resigned—I hear the objection—you accept the lack of clarity, and you want to feel at home in that lack of clarity. Yes, insofar as it's good for my health. What belongs to the present—moving, fluid, persistent—can for a moment be caught in the shapely vessels of thought, but it escapes them at once, leaving empty shards behind. I have committed many errors, but fewer than the others in my circle of acquaintances and friends, because I have moved,

The Rebirth of Utopia: Herbert Marcuse

as it were, obliquely, only appearing to conform, opposing my suspicion ("That's not so") to their arguments and styles. I steered clear of definitions ("So how is it, then?") because things glimmer and vanish, everything is immature, unfulfilled, and has to mature gradually, assume form. The human labyrinth wins my admiration because it develops and expresses what at first is barely sensed. It also develops and expresses every stupidity which has to run its course. The spatial time that separates me from the thirties (which formed me mentally) was full of crimes, the wreck of many hopes, and dazzling technological progress, but that was not all. There were many doors concealed in walls so seemingly uniform that running your hand over them you would not have encountered any roughness on the surface. They could only be opened at the proper moment: then, at the press of a button, unnoticed until then, an entire large section of the wall swung on its axis. Our own powers had not been enough, there had to be some other linkage; that is, a general change had to give the sign that now it could happen. Since that is so, since, in growing, the human labyrinth tends to reveal itself, our desire for meaning is not completely barren. However, to continue the metaphor, there is another uniform wall in front of us now. Even if by touching it here and there I sense points which might be the buttons that open the secret passageways, I am under no obligation to speak of them, for now is not the proper time.

Emigration to America
A Summing Up

For many years I have had variations on the same dream. Uniformed men have blocked the only way out of a tall building and are making arrests, beginning with the lower floors and gradually working their way up to me. Their uniforms are German, or sometimes Russian. Even though the dream is usually composed of fragments of streets and houses from my memory, I do not consider myself a man haunted by nightmares. A recurrent dream is like drawing a bird or a tree after your hand has gotten the feel of it—the realistic features vanish quickly and what remains is a sign, a hieroglyph. I participate in that dream with only a part of myself. Another part of me knows I am just dreaming, that, in a moment, I will wake up.

People who have preserved the capacity for awe are rare —people who can, for instance, still be awed by the earliest, basic human discoveries, like the striking of fire and the shaping of the wheel. No less amazing is the idea that the power of the state should have limits prescribed by law and that nobody should be thrown in prison on the whim of men in uniform. Especially because, while the wheel is here to stay, the protection of law as secured by an independent judiciary is constantly being threatened by the ambition to rule others without any obstacles or checks. Yet only the experience of living in systems where the individual is at the rulers' mercy enables one truly to prize democracy, which submits to the control of the citizenry, albeit incompletely and with reluctance. That is why I have always viewed American rebels with a bit of irony. For them the rule of law is either a cliché, something obvious, a bore, or else it is worthy of hatred and scorn, because the Establishment invokes the law to mask injustice. And, I concede, law, if one has never had to live without it, does not stir our imagination and is much less attractive than slogans calling for a perfect society.

I did not, however, migrate directly to America in 1960 from a totalitarian country, but from France, where, after leaving Poland, I had lived for ten years. With France I had many ties; in the details of its landscape, in the old narrow streets, in wooded dales (like the banks of the rivers L'Isle and Vézère in the Dordogne), I often found reminders of my native Lithuania. Unfortunately, France could not be my home, for reasons which were not only personal but were, as well, indicative of what seems typical of a new migration, the "migration of talents." And so, my views on America are colored not only by my memory of the Eastern parts of Europe but also by my long stay in its Western half.

A certain permanent feature can be observed in the historical existence of particular countries—we might call it the principle of continuity through change, change through continuity. Continuity is so strong in Western Europe that the structures of the nineteenth century seem to persist there unchanged. And those writers who chose the brutality of the struggle for survival as their main theme—Balzac,

Dickens, Zola—are today perhaps less old-fashioned than they appear. The America of Mark Twain or of Upton Sinclair no longer exists, but France, to a considerable extent, is still the France of Balzac; yet, even in the nineteenth century, European and American capitalism were different. The violence of human clashes in America took place on the surface, in the open. The violence in Europe became formalized, coalesced with class divisions hallowed by centuries; it was interiorized, ingrained, or baked in, if one may use such an expression. American capitalism was founded on daring, resourcefulness, largesse, waste; European capitalism was founded on one powerful passion—miserliness. These patterns, which still endure, explain why America succeeded in creating a vast, new sector of the economy adapted to needs that become increasingly evident the closer we come to the twenty-first century: the sector of the universities, research institutes, laboratories, with billions of dollars invested in them. Western Europe, where education has always been the preserve of a narrow elite, failed to produce anything like it. The prodigality of private capital in America made the beginnings possible; money from taxes joined in at the next stage. Miserliness with capital in Europe effectively prevented the laying of foundations for this new sector, and it is doubtful whether the government treasuries will ever be able to overcome the ever-widening gap.

During all the years I lived in Western Europe, I did not have even a single offer from any institution concerned with propagating knowledge. It is true that my field, Slavic literatures, is slightly exotic. Yet one can draw all sorts of conclusions from the fact that it is considered so on a continent at least half of which is occupied by Slavic peoples.

All the truly intelligent people I met during my years in France were European federalists. They were convinced that only the political and economic unification of the lesser powers could offer any sort of counterbalance to both the U.S.A. and Russia. The resistance they encountered, which caused their plans to be implemented very slowly and halfheartedly, was to my mind caused by the same parochial spirit that rejected my qualifications as superfluous, just because I was a newcomer from the other side of the fence. For even though the Slavic domain was beyond the pale of the projected federation, any thinking with breadth and foresight would not write off its closest neighbors. It looked like a weakening of the European will to live—to live as a subject in history. Instead, there was a tacit acquiescence to the role of an object protected by the might of America. I could not help thinking about my being superfluous when Charles de Gaulle proclaimed: "Europe to the Urals"; I simply could not take him seriously.

Besides, it is not Slavic studies that matters here. There were many other educated people unable to find any employment for their skills in the postwar years. Knowledge as a totality of interconnected and interrelated parts is based, to a considerable degree, upon apparently esoteric disciplines; if the spreading of knowledge is considered important, and economically valuable, then ichthyologists, historians of Byzantium, and specialists in Urdu will find places for themselves. The unemployment of the educated, who stagnate in miserable jobs and work in underequipped labs, was humbly accepted as something normal in the France I saw. Quite possibly my observations are somewhat narrow because they are limited to Paris, an exceptionally hard city, but, most likely, they have a larger application.

It is not the bitterness of defeat that speaks in me. If one lives by his pen for ten years, and his books, translated into several foreign languages, have relatively high sales, it is difficult to speak of defeat. It is just that I did not like the profession of European man of letters. My books were translated from Polish, which caused immense difficulties, but I could have reconciled myself to that. The literary profession, however, is more than paper and pen. It also requires abilities like those that had to be possessed by the courtiers who maintained themselves close to the throne of a king or prince by means of carefully thought-out tactics, the game of alliances, and by constantly making themselves known. Now I can smile at the gaffes I made then and could now, without any hostility remaining, draw a portrait of that European publisher upon whose signature so much once depended. That composite portrait would certainly be unjust to some of my well-intentioned employers, though it would also contain certain of their features. This type of book-world potentate is a living contradiction of the maxim "Business is business." His decisions cannot be reduced to calculation, since he publishes what he wants, often exclusively for the honor of the house; his behavior makes you understand that the royalties he pays his authors are not something he owes them but are rather an act of his favor. All that matters is how near you are to his person in the noise and warmth of the beehive he rules. If you are close to him, he is capable of opening his purse and giving you the large sum you need to buy an apartment, undergo a cure, or pay for your daughter's wedding. He can also treat his authors to culinary debauches, picking up checks equal to their annual budget. But it's another story when it comes to normal payments; even modest sums must be squeezed out of him, and his bookkeeping is often submitted to mysterious machinations aimed at lowering his taxes. I simply cannot understand how this type of feudal lord survived in capitalistic enterprises. I noticed no such traits in American publishers, who seem business-like, precise, down-to-earth. Moreover, leaving for America meant I was liberated from literary honoraria as my only source of income. Miracles do happen; they shouldn't, however, be abused.

It was not only the obvious motives forcing so many Western European scholars and scientists to emigrate to America in the last two decades that determined my farewell to Europe. The twentieth century is a century of mass exoduses caused by political upheavals, and their scale was something new, so the formula for adaptation had to be invented by the emigrants themselves. The past did not provide indicators sufficiently valid for the present. No matter how strong the attachment to one's native land, a person can live apart from it only for a limited time if he resists what he sees every day, complaining of the strangeness of a new language, customs, mores, and institutions, straining sight and sound toward his lost fatherland. We are nourished by our senses, and whether we are aware of it or not, the process of ordering our chaotic perceptions and composing them into definite units is constantly at work in us. Total deracination, uprootedness, is contrary to our nature, and the human plant once plucked from the ground tries to sink roots into the ground onto which it was thrown. This happens because we are physical beings; that is, we occupy space, and the space we occupy, bounded by the surface of our skin, cannot be located in a "nowhere." Just as our hand reaches out and picks up a pencil lying on a table, thus establishing a relationship between our body and what is outside it, our imagination extends us, establishing a sensory and visual relationship between us and a street, a town, a district, and a country. In exiles from the Eastern part of Europe one often notices a desperate refusal to accept that fact; they try to preserve their homeland as an ideal space in which they dwell and move, yet since it exists only in memory and is not reinforced by everyday impressions, it becomes rigid, transformed into words that grow more obstinate the more their tangible contents fade.

That I grew into France with my five senses was understandable, since, in spite of all the differences between its various provinces, Europe is a whole shaped by a common past. Nevertheless, the choice confronting one in France was not to my liking—you can be either a Frenchman or a foreigner. Actually, there is no choice at all, since Frenchness has a nearly metaphysical character in no way connected with length of residence or passport. My accent marked me with the stigma of foreignness, just as certain old Parisian taxi drivers, eternal émigrés, were marked. I was never once mistaken when, after a few words of French, I spoke to them in Russian. That accent, however, was mine, my property, and I made no attempt to rid myself of it, just as I made no attempt to rid myself of my old attachments and loyalties. This was not frowned upon, but only because foreigners were forgiven all their eccentricities. It is difficult to grasp how much such exclusion interferes with the ordering activity of the imagination, which attempts to assimilate the province of Dordogne, to take one example, so that it is "mine" and not something outside me, the temporary property of the tourist. In America my impulse to feel at home, an ordinary, normal, healthy impulse, did not encounter any such obstacles, because here everything was just the other way around; my Slavic accent, my coming from a distant country, the indestructible habits and reflexes which excluded me permanently in France, made me normal here, one of many in a crowd of newcomers, "American" precisely because I did not have to renounce anything.

Our thinking is always imprisoned by notions which at one point arose from reality but which later lead an autonomous life, out of step with the present. Immigration to America in the second half of our century is not the same as it was in the nineteenth century, not even what it was a few decades ago. The last spiritual remnants of the epoch of the steam engine are already disintegrating and dying out; man has found himself before something still unnamed, and though his consciousness lags behind general transformations, he does perceive that everything now happening to our entire species is enormous, ominous, and perhaps ultimate. This is not the first time in the history of civilization that men have experienced crisis, disintegration, a sense of the end. Many generations lived with it in Imperial Rome, probably something similar oppressed the medieval millenarians; the Renaissance was clear and bright in appearance only—in fact, it labored to achieve classical order in the face of its own dark reflections on the loss of the traditional certainties, hierarchies, virtues. When America's suffering, the violence of its nearly insoluble conflicts, America's uncertainty, are seen against the background of this new large crisis, America's fate loses that peculiarity its elemental growth in colonizing the continent once possessed in the eyes of Europe. The destructive influence of technology on the popular religious imagination, automation, the spread of education, man's fear of self-destruction through the gradual or sudden poisoning of nature, show the universal features of the American adventure—it condenses and exemplifies what has overtaken or is now overtaking people all over the world. There is no turning back from the discovery of fire and the discovery of the wheel. Similarly, there is no turning back the chain-reaction consequences of modern knowledge, though here and there, for various local reasons, they are slowed down. Sometimes, too, a whole complex of interconnected factors, spiritual, technical, and social, clear the way from beneath in spite of some obligatory ideology. Since self-accusation and the feeling of being lost are more out in the open in America than anywhere else, America is the testing ground for all mankind. It is also possible that the corrosive tone and the alliances between revolutionaries and bohemians are the price a materially powerful country must pay in the process of transforming itself into a country of poetic and philosophic enterprises.

As to my homelessness, it is what makes my integration into America easier, because its inhabitants have always suffered from homelessness and uprootedness, later called alienation (for who besides the Indians was not an alien?). With the exception of the farming areas on the East Coast, which were colonized earlier, the wanderers and settlers had to master and order the space surrounding them everywhere, not only in the literal sense but through their imagination, which was at work both when they were awake and when they were asleep. If only this had led to moving from one residence to another, permanent one, but no, not even that was allowed by the mobility demanded by industrial society. No wonder that the very core of American literature has always been the question: "Who am I?" The individual establishes his identity physically, by relating himself to objects within the reach of his hands and eyes. Through his expanding perception he extends his own identity, first spatially, to include a village, a district, a country, then temporally, into his country's past, which must be somehow accessible to him, graspable in its details, lest he be "nowhere." Where that is not possible, substitutes are sought, which is what Walt Whitman did when he borrowed the French expression *"en masse,"* and applied it to the American scene. If I am *en masse,* I do not set out to define myself in terms of my knight's castle, peasant's hut, or burger's store, I am Everyman and I must define myself in a universal fluidity, in a human collective in motion, composed of Everymen. This is superhumanly difficult, because the distinctive features supporting and aiding my individuality disappear or are rendered universal and therefore neutral; for instance, what is closest to my body, my clothes, no longer functions as a sign of belonging to one group as opposed to another. The "I" is then seen from outside as if it were an item in a store window, which contradicts its self-contained uniqueness. I am not speaking here about dissolving into the mass, or about communion through temperature and rhythm (it is characteristic that in Europe Whitman was read as the bard of mass meetings and marches), but rather about relating oneself to other individuals who have been thrown in the same geographically shaky position I have. As far back as one hundred years ago, the *"masse"* was a "lonely crowd."

Human particles were torn from their ground earlier and

on a larger scale in America than anywhere else, and this made America the unintentional precursor of modern life. This was to be generalized due to the late arrival of the industrial revolution in many countries, as well as to their wars and political upheavals. This land of the exile became almost a paradigm of all exile, and especially of the exile from a mental space made hierarchic by the Throne of God. European civilization was founded on certain spatial equivalents of religious truths. These were vertical patterns —Heaven, Earth, Hell—as well as horizontal—the perilous travels of knights in search of the Grail, the legend of the Crusades fighting for the tomb of Christ, or journeys on treacherous roads illustrating the soul's slow advance toward salvation despite devilish temptation. Even a sixteenth-century Polish treatise in verse, *The Raftsman* by Klonowic, on the transportation of wheat by river barge, is, at times, an allegory of the temporal pilgrimage of a Christian to the desired harbor. Quite different images appear when people try to express their disorientation in a space rendered inert by the collapse of religious faith. This space is not subject to the will, it is useless, senseless, as are the wastelands of huge cities, garbage dumps, vacant lots covered with scrap metal and overgrown with nettles, a kind of limbo once supposedly inhabited by souls who knew neither Good nor Evil. In the two most representative plays of the theater of the absurd, Beckett's *Waiting for Godot* and *Beautiful Days*, the action takes place in a "nowhere," material forms are only symbols of aimless time closing circularly upon itself. But because of its elemental yet anti-organic growth, America created landscapes of refuse, dumps, slums, neon wildernesses, before the artistic imagination concerned itself with them, so that without exaggeration one can say that an unstable space contradicting our desire for order serves here as scenery for a play, but not one performed on stage—a play whose characters are Everyman and Everyman. The peoples of other continents assimilate the products of American culture with ease because American reality does not have to metaphorize reality overmuch, and is itself a metaphor, revealing man's disinheritance.

One of my civilization's constant ingredients is a complaint of loss, a nostalgic dream turned toward the past, idealizing an ancient harmony with nature, primeval innocence, the full integration into a tribal community, a hieratic space spread between rural towns and heaven. It goes hand in hand with a rage against the world to which we were born, growing imperceptibly into a rage against existence in general. The contrast between the historically unprecedented achievements of technology and medicine, which are basically favorable to the human milieu, and such gloomy states of mind is quite enigmatic, all the more so since the fear of a final catastrophe (atomic war, the pollution of the oceans), which may or may not occur, seems to be only a mask for an illness more profound and more difficult to name. "The impossibility of living" that so oppresses young Americans, among others, probably testifies, as has previously been the case, to the exhaustion of some spiritual resources and to a feeling of hanging between something which is ending and something which has not yet begun. An American philosopher, José Ferrater Mora, wrote about the Roman schools of Stoics, Cynics, and Platonists almost as if they were our contemporaries, because they were all searching for salvation, trying to stay sane in a society they saw as chaotic and on which an individual could have little influence. It was probably their works which, much later, when the medieval order was "out of joint," Hamlet studied at Wittenberg—though he, in his moment of truth, did not limit himself to withdrawal but, to his grief, decided to cure the evil in Elsinore castle.

Although today there is a tendency to exaggerate the exceptional nature of our situation, our "epoch" began somewhere around the end of the eighteenth, the beginning of the nineteenth century, and should be viewed as a whole. It is distinguished by a central philosophical problem ripening slowly as a result of the criticism directed at traditional Christian beliefs and aristocratic institutions, monarchy chief among them. This is the problem of political terror, which, if used intelligently, will permit the conscious and the pure to achieve the redemption and deification of man. There is a close, fundamental link between all the varieties of nihilistic despair at a world unredeemed by God, a world empty because abandoned by Providence, where good and evil are deprived of higher sanction, and that impulse of the will postulating reason in opposition to universal unreason. The true revolutionaries were the poets and the artists, even the most ethereal and least bloodthirsty of them, because they cleared the way; that is, they acted as the organizers of the collective imagination in a new dimension, that of man's solitude as a species. Hence, the obliteration of the boundary between bohemian artists and advocates of political action. In European romanticism one can see the collapse of the ideal space that suited both man's rootedness in his native village and the aspirations of the soul striving for heaven. Space became dynamic, it eludes the "now" because the "now" is condemned as unbearable, and, by the nature of things, fuses with spatial images of

historical time. It is not true that romantics only turn their
eyes nostalgically to the past, dreaming of medieval castles,
knights, and minstrels; other romantics made efforts at
prophecy, since both the former and the latter (often one
and the same) prefer the past and future—any movement
away—to their own dimension. The connection with the
dynamic elements of Christianity (the Messiah, the expectation of a Second Coming) and with the evolutionism
of the biological sciences has impelled them and their
successors to a belief in Progress, but, in the final analysis,
this has been exploited by the most fervent and the
most logical, who denied that progress is automatic and
opposed that concept with acts of conscious will that trans-
form the face of the earth. Political terror has an honorable
genealogy; it focuses all the most complicated problems,
and Dostoevsky was probably right when he posed the
either-or dilemma—the God-man or the man-God. And
so an improved (improved by Marx and his disciples) and
more fully theoretical version of the terror-salvation of the
virtuous Jacobins became the crowning achievement of
Europe's spiritual quest. A change *en masse*, different from
America's, produced a directionally oriented space. The
temporal pilgrimage of the soul on the narrow way amid
snares and abysses was replaced by the march of nations
from the Egyptian bondage of capitalism across a desert of
(temporary) privation and (temporary) terror, guided by
commander-priests, a process otherwise known as the building of socialism (to be done brick by brick, nineteenth-
century style).

Western Europe's fate was to export and to be conquered by what it had exported. Its body fled overseas from
the congealed, formalized violence of the struggle for exis-

tence, preferring homelessness and hope to home and hopelessness. Its spirit betrayed continental tendencies and operated on both sides of the Urals. When the fall finally occurred and power shifted to America and Russia, it looked like a fable with a moral. There is a saying: Don't talk about rope in the home of a hanged man. The Europe in which I lived after the war tried to pretend there was no rope. It dreamed of a return both to a style of life and to those intellectual premises whose conclusions had been drawn elsewhere.

America was first Europeanized technologically and surpassed Europe at once. Now America is being Europeanized again. Obviously, universal education and the respect for literature and art inculcated by the host of intellectuals employed by colleges, universities, and research institutes can only mean that all sorts of European ideas, along with their internal logic of development, are being grafted onto the native tree. Similarly, the Greece that was grafted onto a not particularly sophisticated Rome was not limited to Homer or Pindar; on the contrary, the Romans also absorbed all of decadent Hellenistic thought and art.

The commercial efficiency of the mass media—which put a premium on garishness, brutality, sex, a nearly suicidal freedom of expression under the pretext of art—and the particular features of American schools provide the young generation with something that can only be called exercises in nihilism. The raising of the young without indoctrination is something new—until now there have always been attempts to indoctrinate them with a religion or a socialistic or nationalistic creed; however, American educators themselves have no fundamental beliefs from which to proceed. According to Herbert Marcuse, this lack of any direction constitutes an insidious and covert preparation for a bestial existence reduced to earning and spending. Yet Marcuse only represents the European post-nihilist phase; that is, he speaks for man, who first lost his imagination and his metaphysically grounded values, which could order and structure space, and who then decided to turn to society and to postulate values themselves, assuming that social space could be made rational and transparent only by political terror. Thus, Marcuse's quarrel with America is actually a quarrel with some undefined "opening up" to what is called culture, something in which bourgeois Europe was well versed, though on a more modest scale. That "opening up" usually resulted in all ideas becoming of equal importance and utterly relative, while, in practice, sonority and range were granted only to those ideas that helped shape the attitudes of bitterness, despair, and the sense of man's superfluousness in the universe. This usually resulted either in the acceptance of getting and spending or, among bohemians, in the worship of Art with a capital A as the only absolute. And as well, in the next phase, a longing for political terror.

The lack of indoctrination today is not only an "opening up" but, as well, a submission to a certain unplanned propaganda. The mass media are like a magic ring that allows you to see in an instant all the suffering, all the oppression, all the injustice in America and the whole world. The good, the triumph of the human will, and persistence are excluded as insufficiently exciting and commercially weak. Scientific discoveries, the construction of gigantic dams, bridges, freeways, achievements which, in totalitarian countries, would have been trumpeted as historic events, get a few lines of print or ten seconds on television—who cares about such ordinary, boring things? Of course, in America there is the tragedy of the ghettos, there is much injustice and poverty, but there was more a half century ago; then, however, our consciousness was not in contact with them every day. The earth has always been full of human suffering, but the inhabitants of self-enclosed communities and regions had no way of embracing them all simultaneously. The anger of the moralists who are now rebelling against evil provides the justification for orgies of masochism. Blind, emotional protest blurs the distinction between lesser and greater evils. An honest college president who opposes the utterly senseless demands of the students is publicly denounced as a Hitler or an Eichmann; the President of the country is presented in a play as Macbeth with bloody hands, his wife as Lady Macbeth. In such a mental climate, it is hardly surprising that political terror begins to be seen as positive and that it is considered inappropriate to reflect upon how much one gains or loses by employing it.

My seasoning in Europe's nihilistic diversions, and my awareness of their results, does not allow me to sympathize with the conformism of moans and maledictions obligatory for American intellectuals, who are, on the whole, remarkably well supplied with worldly goods. Their conformism is so far advanced that they are sometimes reminiscent of Pantagruel's sheep, and to convince oneself of this, it is enough to read the periodicals they edit, which are designed to their taste. To resist that fashion with irony may be something of an obligation for me, but great difficulties arise when certain dubious theses, well worth checking, are accepted in the dominant spiritual climate as self-evident.

The contradiction that exists between our desire that the

human world be transparent and rational and some law invalidating or postponing reasonable plans is real and not illusory. That contradiction becomes particularly acute when we confront extreme dangers requiring quick and radical remedies; for example, the destruction of the natural environment, which is turning whole regions of America into wastelands and dumps, and the struggle, rarely won, for laws directed against private interests. If an individual sees what would be rational and yet is powerless, he begins to feel that existence is opaque and absurd, and that in turn leads to dreams of political terror, which, for the most part, find vicarious expression in the violent tone of poems, novels, and paintings. Though the progressive intelligentsia in tsarist Russia had completely different problems, their pattern of thought was not very different from that of their young American cousins of today. Nonsense had to be changed into sense, corruption had to be cured by force. Unfortunately, that intelligentsia was to learn that the victory of political terror drove out one absurdity only to replace it with another, and that nothing could be less transparent than the bureaucratic jungle.

I have no idea how the American system works, nor do I understand how the pragmatic mind operates. It's quite possible that it has some loathing for logical sequences of the sort "if *a*, then *b*; if *b*, then *c*," as well as for any planning in advance; it always begins dealing with urgent problems at the last possible moment (if not five minutes too late), under utmost constraint. Thus far, that collective organism's ability to assimilate the unforeseen has been quite remarkable. I happened to have been a witness to conflicts which, to my European mind, seemed impossible to conclude by agreement. I have, however, maintained a foreigner's reticence in relation to the talents for procrastination and parliamentary compromise which have been developed here, because I was conscious of my own limitations. In an attempt to find a name for what set me apart, I came to the conclusion that it was a tendency to argue from some basis—that is, an inclination to abstraction—which deprived many of my judgments of their usefulness, and even more, perhaps, by my shame at making concessions, though no one around me was ashamed to, if the disposition of forces required that concessions be made. And so the framework for terroristic endeavors was, to some extent, prepared in advance, and those endeavors were assigned the role of extracting privileges by blackmail; here it seems that the masters of American politics are the children, because they discovered how so effectively to terrorize their parents that they would even allow them to jump off the roof for a moment's peace and quiet. Whatever is shocking, offensive, horrifying, works, and the fact that it works commercially, as well, is of no small importance. A significant portion of Europe's radical bohemian ideas, recorded in the history of modern art, were a response to the omnipotence of the market. *Pour épater le bourgeois* indicated the only way to his pocket. Similarly, today's American "underground press" would not sell if it did not surpass the Surrealists in the macabre and in consciously cultivated vileness, and if half its staff weren't trying to pass themselves off as reincarnations of Che Guevara. The profitability of protest does not preclude the sincerity of certain hostile feelings, but, still, it does turn intellectual fashions into theater, exactly the opposite of the seriousness of the Russians in the tsarist empire.

We know nothing certain about the callings of nations, and time and again only touch and blindly feel the principal constants recurring over the course of decades, or a century. Often it seems to me that the vocation of America consists of a duality encountered nowhere else—the duality of desperation and success. I have a distant predecessor in emigration to this continent, Julian Ursyn Niemcewicz, who came to these shores in 1796. He was a man of the Enlightenment, an enemy of autocratic monarchies and an enthusiast of the American republic. He took a moderate position in the great quarrel of that time about the French Revolution—he sympathized with it in its beginnings, then, in the period of the terror, cooled considerably. In his *Travels in America* published in English translation as *Under Their Vine and Fig Tree*, he recorded his visit with a well-to-do farmer, a hardy citizen who irritated him by complaining about widespread stagnation and apathy. As was often to occur with refugees from Europe in conversations with despairing American moralists, Niemcewicz fell silent and noted for himself:

"We must have a revolution," says Mr. Logan. "That alone can save us: but would you believe it, our people do not want to hear talk of it. They are already corrupted. Ah! if I were now in France, if I might see all that goes on there, how I would rejoice." "Madman," I said to myself, "you do not know what you want; you have a large and comfortable house, fields which give you four times your need. You live under wise and free laws and pine after upheaval and blood. You are a fanatic, my friend, your brain is sick. The tranquillity, the abundance with which you live weighs you down; you feel the need of being aroused and shaken up, even if it means the ruin of your house or of your country. But go to France, go to Europe, see what goes on there and you will return cured of your madness."

When I was a student in Wilno, then part of Poland, any sobriety of thought or skepticism about the magnificent slogans promising total solutions made us angry and ashamed; these weaknesses had to be stifled. Now, when I look back with some perspective, I must admit that reason was always the loser, as if confirming that its advice is valid only for individuals and not for human collectives. Yet it was the loser only in the relatively short run, for, in fact, only the individual is real, not the mass movements in which he voluntarily loses himself in order to escape himself. I have never considered myself a political writer and have no ambition to save America or the world. Here, now, I am only asking myself what I have learned in America, and what I value in that experience. I can boil it all down to three sets of pros and cons: for the so-called average man, against the arrogance of intellectuals; for the Biblical tradition, against the search for individual or collective nirvana; for science and technology, against dreams of primeval innocence.

My self-education has profited, I hope, from living in avant-garde California. Here one must come to terms with one's own pride. In his optimistic moments, every writer considers himself a genius, and if he lives in his own small country, whose language differs from its neighbors', there will be no lack of support for his favorite self-image. Writing in America in Polish (for the poet can use only the language of his childhood), I deprive myself of that comfort. But, in fact, it is not language, or, as in France, being an alien, that is important. As a result of America's vast-

ness and human mass, the bonds between a poet and his au-
dience are different than they are where I came from;
besides, those bonds have always been very strong in Slavic
countries. So I must simply state that I am one of many poets
in the San Francisco Bay area. Most of them write in English, but there are also those who write in Spanish, Greek,
German, Russian. Even if one has some renown, he is, in
his everyday dealings with people, anonymous, and so is,
again, one among many, but in another, larger sense.
Whatever satisfies our vanity becomes a very effective *divertissement*, of the kind to which men resort, according to
Pascal, to veil the futility of our endeavors and our fear of
death. At least one *divertissement*, the most important one,
recognition, is rarely attainable in America, where we are
all particles of a lonely crowd. Probably the inhabitants of
cosmopolitan Greek-Jewish-Latin Rome felt something
similar. I do not mean at all to say that I am above such
trifles as the desire for fame and recognition, but America
pushes you to the wall and compels a kind of stoic virtue:
to do your best and at the same time to preserve a certain
detachment that derives from an awareness of the ignorance, childishness, and incompleteness of all people,
oneself included.

"Of all people." I am fed up with dividing people into
those few who know and the dull masses who don't realize
what is useful for them. I have no desire to be one of the
elect dragging the masses by force to Utopia. Youth
brought up in affluence, masquerading in beggars' clothing
and revolutionary ideas, commands less of my respect than
hardworking lumberjacks, miners, bus drivers, bricklayers,
whose mentality arouses scorn in the young. Perhaps this is
the much-ridiculed mentality of the Bible-reading Ameri-

can entrenched in self-righteousness; and yet the fact that America is still a country of the Bible has, and will continue to have, lasting consequences. No matter how deeply religious beliefs have been eroded, the King James Version is the heart of the language, it determined its literary development, and the work of Whitman, Melville, and their successors constantly refers us back to it. The Bible is the common property of believers, agnostics, atheists. Anyone who knows from experience, as I do, how important certain of the less obvious human virtues can be will not frivolously call a certain heavy decency and unselfishness plain stupidity, even if they are accompanied by mental limitations. Nor will he shrug off the clash of goodness and wickedness which originates in the Bible. In spite of arguments to the contrary, in spite of the paradox of brutal and cruel deeds producing unintended good results, or perhaps just because of that paradox, America is the legitimate heir to the Judeo-Christian civilization, summoned to the technical works which that civilization, alone among all others, has rendered possible. Therefore, it was just and beautiful that the American astronauts flying over the surface of the moon addressed the inhabitants of Earth with an old message, the beginning of the Book of Genesis.

The disruption of the hierarchy connecting the separate areas of our activity is one of the causes of the present chaos in thought. The human labyrinth grows more and more complex, and language changes from connective tissue into a superior power, whether it be a language of words, or one transmitted electronically, or one composed of masses and spots of color. Considering the autonomous, insane expansion of language, we don't even know whether we have the right to use the notions "literature" and "art," which may be obsolete; but, since the nineteenth century, when they took that track, people have expected revelations from language. Yet our fate does not depend on what was once called *humaniora*, but on religion and science. Fortunately, both the America of the Bible and the America of technology remind me of this fact, despite my professional aberrations as a humanist. The tomorrow we would like for planet Earth—justice, peace, the elimination of hunger and poverty—is not very likely unless a fundamental conversion occurs. There have always been a multitude of preachers calling for inner rebirth, a rebirth of the heart, and, all told, this has been no help against cruelty and injustice. My friends would think I had lost my mind if I began making evangelical pronouncements. I am not, however, in the least counting on some effort of the will, but rather on something independent of the will—data which would order our spatial imagination anew.

There is no halting the imagination, which tends to compose everything we learn about the cosmos and man into harmonious symbol-enhanced systems; i.e., world views. If one of those systems is lost, the imagination either moves in a void, creating images of heartbreaking senselessness (which is itself a kind of sense, but a negative one), or it sets about introducing order by making use of the materials at its disposal. Without any shame, let us admit we are children facing a disordered heap of blocks; no child can resist the desire of his hand to express the need of his mind. Political and social ideas cannot be examined in themselves because they are links in a chain of a few basic images. The ideas that are today an active force arose from the disintegration of the pre-Copernican system. That was a static system in which Heaven exerted an upward pull and Hell a pull downward, and where evil, in a sense, had been tamed, since its dosage could not vary. That system was superseded by a dynamic one in which the "withdrawal" of God did not necessarily mean the renunciation of heaven, for now space became the movement of providential, redeeming time—hell was the present, heaven the future. Before anyone sees these statements as only my obsessions, let him consider for a moment the current concerns of Catholic theologians. They noticed, belatedly, that the religious truths which fit the pre-Copernican system encounter the unconscious resistance of even the most zealous Christians, so they began to make them dynamic, introducing images of humanity's march through time, of diminishing evil, of history as a Christological process—to such an extent that some Catholic catechisms open with chapters that seem straight from textbooks on material and moral evolution. This is legitimate, since the "divine pedagogy" that regulates movement is at the very heart of Judeo-Christianity, in contrast to the cyclical vision of the Egyptians and Greeks. It is hard, however, not to notice that this sudden zeal is an attempt on the part of the theologians to adapt themselves to shifts in the collective imagination, which occurred outside the church, without its participation, and against its intent. Competing with lay progressives in providing solace, they sometimes go as far as considering it tactless to mention the devil. Evil has no weight at all, because by the time it is recognized, it already belongs to the past (but what about the innocent people tortured to death to bring about the glorious future?). Many pronouncements by high-ranking Catholic figures sound as if they came from the socialists of a hundred years ago, those noble-minded dreamers who were, back then, treated by the Church with disapproval, to say the least. It seems there are few ways out of nihilistic inertia, and that only one is at hand—a leap into the future, a denial of the evil present. An American hippie switching to political action and the clergyman who wants to win him over by proclaiming to all and sundry his social fervor travel the same road.

The dynamic model is with us and is here to stay. The old argument of the conservatives that since man is a corrupt creature, the earth is and will be a vale of tears, that *Plus ça change, plus c'est la même chose*" does not entirely convince us. Yet it is difficult to rid oneself of the suspicion that the imagination, if it is able to maintain some sort of equilibrium only as long as it rushes forward, outdistancing time, is resorting to surrogates; that it is motivated not so much by belief in a better humanity as by a loathing for the nothingness and chaos in which it must remain until it leaps the distance between today and some hypothetical tomorrow. That covert motivation may encourage grasping at straws, even the most stupid and inhuman ideologies. Instances of skillfully maintained self-deceit are so numerous in our epoch that it is not even worthwhile to cite examples. So the question is whether the wise evaluation of programs and plans does not primarily mean finding a spiritual home in the here and now. If there is any hope, it is only because those images of the universe and of our fate in it, which are simply unbearable for man, seem to be the belated heritage of Newton's concept of the great mechanism, while the new elements are still scattered and have not been integrated.

In spite of the internal erosion of the various denominations, religion may be in a (potentially) better situation today than it was a hundred years ago. The thousands of works in anthropology and psychology, the thousands of studies of myths and symbols in literature, suffuse the collective consciousness with a sort of humble amazement at the archetypes that take shape in religion and at the vague outlines of something that can only be called an unchanging human nature. This makes syncretism tempting, and here there is another similarity with Imperial Rome, where, at a certain moment, the cult of Mithras, Manichaeism, the Gnostics, and Christianity all coexisted. Also, the skeptical mind of the European Enlightenment treated all religions equally by subjecting them to the control of reason. Today, however, everyone is struck by the total strangeness and mysteriousness of the human being, a being who lives underground, only partially protruding through the surface, and therefore the "rationality" of religions does not suffice as a criterion, the scales tip, rather, toward faith as the secret of individual freedom and individual destiny. At the same time, ritual, which had been a dead letter for the rationalistically inclined generations, begins to acquire more value, for it is not only in the theater that Everyman is dependent on "interhuman space" or, as Witold Gombrowicz called it, the "interhuman church": people already know that they are always "infecting" each other with their gestures, looks, and words. A ritual constructs a sacral space among those present at it. Hence, not only have radical attempts at renewing the liturgy in churches and at private gatherings emerged, but also ecstatic ceremonies, which might not seem very religious but which are in fact related to the liturgy.

As to the influence of science, it operates on the lag principle, spreading slowly like a drop of water on a blotter. Science acts upon the imagination either directly, or indirectly through technology, but in neither case immediately, and at least half of ourselves is trapped in eighteenth- and nineteenth-century space. We cannot even hope to guess what space will be like for our descendants; at best, we can collect signs and omens—uncertain, encoded by the very roundabout nature of gradual transformations. It's a bit like looking at the earth from the moon. Beginning with Jules Verne, the authors of science fiction have made this sight familiar to us, but truly to see, as we now have, our huge, round, blue home is qualitatively different, though we cannot say why. Perhaps something tugs at our hearts, some inkling that the earth was, after all, destined to be the center, as it was before Copernicus, and that the geocentric and anthropocentric vision does not merit derision? Instead of anger at existence, did we perhaps for a moment feel love for good water, good trees, good plants? Or did the morality play of the absurd, which supposedly portrays the human condition faithfully, make us ashamed, because, juxtaposed to the cosmic ballet, it revealed its dependence on one transient variety of sensibility, as do the clothes of 1880? Besides, it is not only interplanetary voyages that are imperceptibly reconstructing the imagination, but also the heterogeneity of times; the multiplicity of possible spaces; so-called primitive man's incredible complexity of mind—everything science reveals, changing reality from a mechanism into a crystal cabinet of wonders, with reflections flashing from mirror to mirror. Not long ago, science was accustomed to reduction; it used to "explain" the miraculous as "only" the simple consequences of certain causes. Today manifold increases have replaced reductions, and the laboratory makes space as sublime and magical as a fairy tale about elves.

So much is happening all at once that to guess what is repetition and what is augury is practically impossible. The complexity and chameleon-like mutability hidden behind seemingly tangible forms is now spreading across the entire earth, and to write about the present is to behave like the blind man who, touching the elephant's trunk, proclaimed that the elephant is long and snake-like. I am certain only of my amazement. Amazement that something like America exists, and that humanity still exists, though it should have exterminated itself long ago or perished from starvation, from epidemics, or from the poisons it excretes. But amazement induces silent contemplation, and whenever I take up my pen, which itself pretends to knowledge, since language is composed of affirmations and negations, I treat that act only as the exorcism of the evil spirits of the present.